SUPERPOTENCY

SUPERPOTENCY

How to get it, use it, and
maintain it for a lifetime

■

Dudley Seth Danoff, M.D., F.A.C.S.

WARNER BOOKS

A Time Warner Company

This book is not intended as a substitute for medical advice. The reader should regularly consult a physician in matters relating to his or her health and particularly with respect to any symptoms that may require diagnosis or medical attention.

This book contains many references to actual cases the author has encountered over the years. However, names and other identifying characteristics have been changed to protect the privacy of those involved.

Warner Books, Inc., 1271 Avenue of the Americas, New York, NY 10020
W A Time Warner Company

Printed in the United States of America
First printing: January 1993
10 9 8 7 6 5 4 3 2 1

Library of Congress Cataloging-in-Publication Data

Danoff, Dudley Seth.
  Superpotency / Dudley Seth Danoff.
    p.   cm.
  Includes index.
  ISBN 0-446-51623-6
  1. Penis. 2. Masculinity (Psychology) 3. Impotence. I. Title.
QP257.D36 1993
612.6'1—dc20   91-51166
                                                                        CIP

Book design: H. Roberts

To the memory of my father, Alfred,
my lifelong pal, a loving husband
and true man of penis power

ACKNOWLEDGMENTS

I would like to express my gratitude to all those who helped make this project a reality: to my many patients who shared their stories and thoughts with me, teaching me things I could never learn in books; to my close friend Norman Brokaw, who was the first to believe that my somewhat unorthodox ideas would make a worthwhile book; to Nanscy Neiman, who had the courage to change her mind and lend her enthusiasm and good judgment to the project; to Susan Suffes, for her astute editorial contributions; to Phil Goldberg, who often found the right words for many of my ideas and helped structure the raw material into book form.

My deepest appreciation goes to my family: to my children, Aurele and Doran, for understanding why I was even busier than usual and excusing my absences from ballet recitals and soccer games; and to my wife, Hedva, for her patience and support, for convincing me that the book would appeal to women as much as men, and for helping me understand the woman's point of view.

CONTENTS

PREFACE

Superpotency is a response to a disturbing observation I have made while practicing urology for the past two decades: large numbers of American men suffer from what I call penis weakness. Insecurity and uncertainty about sexual performance is depriving them and their partners of complete enjoyment and satisfaction. I wrote the book to replace ignorance and mythology with factual information, and self-doubt with confidence. My goal is to help every man achieve superpotency. To put it another way, I want to help them maximize their penis power—the greatest gift that nature has bestowed upon males.

As a busy urologic surgeon in Beverly Hills, I have seen more than 100,000 penises in my professional lifetime. While each is unique, just as hands and feet are unique, they are also remarkably alike anatomically. But there is an enormous variation in how they function in their sexual capacity. Over the years I have observed that these differences have very little to do with penis anatomy, or with a man's size and looks, or his level of success, wealth, and status. It has mainly to do with how he *perceives* his penis. In addition to its other functions, the penis is an organ of expression. What gives it its power is much more than the condition of its blood vessels and nerves.

Penis power is the power of positive thinking as applied to your penis.

Your penis is what you think it is. It's as big as you think it is. It's as reliable as you think it is. It's as potent as you think it is. That is my basic message.

The book contains everything you need to know—based on my medical observations—to help you achieve your full sexual potential. Although one of my goals is to educate the public and bring the penis out of the closet, this is not a textbook. There is nothing overly technical in these pages. Rather, in straightforward, easily understood terms I have covered the facts I consider essential for the layperson to know about the penis and related organs. The amount that even well-educated, sophisticated people don't know about the penis is shocking. Even more shocking is what they *think* is true but is not.

This book is not a psychology text either. Plenty of writers have given us lengthy analyses of male sexuality and treatises on the treatment of sexual dysfunction. My purpose is less academic. I am concerned with the average man who is mystified or confused about his penis and wants to get better use out of it. I am concerned about his attitude and beliefs, not his upbringing, his toilet training, or his inner child. Nor is this a how-to book or a sex manual in the usual sense, although you will find a great many practical tips in these pages, including valuable exercises for improving your penis power.

In sum, I have written the book that I, as a man and practicing urologist, wish had been written a long time ago. It would have saved a lot of men from self-doubt and humiliation; it would have saved a lot of women from sexual frustration; and it would have saved a lot of marriages, period.

In writing the book I imagined myself speaking directly to a male reader. However, it is my fervent wish that as many women read it as men. I have never met a woman who did not want to maximize the penis power of the man in her life. The book will give female readers a greater understanding of men in general and the ability to derive utmost satisfaction with their partners. Chapter Twelve is addressed specifically to women. However, to avoid repetition I did not include important information covered earlier in the book that readers of both sexes should have. Therefore, I urge all women to read the entire book. It was written for both sexes. The issues dealt with are pertinent to all men and the women in their lives.

There is much in these pages that will surprise you. Some of it might even shock or outrage you. I welcome whatever controversy might ensue, for I stand fully behind my observations and offer them with one purpose only: to end the plague of penis weakness, with its attendant cynicism, despair, and frustration. Superpotency is not a luxury, it is the natural birthright of every man. Its full exercise will render all our lives—male and female, young and old—more vigorous, more healthy, and more enjoyable in every respect. If you follow the advice in this book you will find that every aspect of your life—work, play, relationships—will be enriched. Superpotency elevates the mind, the heart, and the spirit, not just the penis. The man who has it is blessed, and so is the woman with whom he shares it.

The aim of medicine is to let our patients
die young as late as possible.
　　　　　—Hippocrates (460–377 B.C.)

SUPERPOTENCY

1
Penis Power

In the twenty-three years I have been practicing urology, I have treated every conceivable problem in the male genitourinary and reproductive systems, from minor herpes to major bladder infections, from kidney transplants to prostate cancer. I have treated men so rich they could buy the hospital in which I did their surgery, and men so poor they couldn't purchase aspirin, let alone pay for their operation. I have treated world-famous celebrities and the guys who shine celebrities' shoes or fix their sinks. I have treated geniuses and dunces, Ph.D.'s and dropouts, men who have read everything and men who can't read their names. I have treated the young, the middle-aged, and the elderly; straights, gays, and bisexuals; married men, single men, divorced men, and widowers; the promiscuous, the monogamous, and the celibate. All that experience has taught me that, despite the vast differences among them, men have certain things in common. Three of my observations led directly to this book:

1. To a far greater extent than we have acknowledged, men are penis-oriented. In the minds of men, the penis reigns supreme.

2. Most men (and, of course, women even more so) are woefully ignorant about penises and the male sexual apparatus in general.

1

3. An alarming percentage of men are plagued by penis weakness or penis insecurity.

Let's look at each of those points separately.

MEN ARE PENIS-ORIENTED CREATURES

By penis-oriented I mean that a man's personality, behavior, and outlook on life are governed in large part by his image of his penis and by the signals his penis sends him. Usually, the suggestion that a particular man is penis-driven contains pejorative connotations. We say things like, "His big head is ruled by his little head" or "His brains are in his weiner." But I don't mean it pejoratively. I am asserting, as a fact of life, the dominance of the penis. It goes to extremes with Don Juans, or exhibitionists, or men who are obsessed by sex, but those are not the only ones who are penis-driven. So is the average man, and there is nothing wrong with that. It is simply the way things are. In many respects, the penis is the organ of a man's soul. It is the axis around which the male body and personality rotate.

The truth of my observation is reflected in part in our rich heritage of bawdy humor. Is any body part the subject of more jokes than the penis? Not likely. And much of that humor directly reflects my point about the supremacy of the organ. For example, a man says to his girlfriend, "Women don't have brains," to which she replies, "That's because we don't have penises to put them in." Then there is the riddle a woman patient recently told me: What do you call the superfluous skin around the penis? Answer: A man.

That the penis is central to a man's identity is also indicated by the number of nicknames that have been assigned to it. Do we have nicknames for arms and legs and livers? Not even buttocks and breasts come close to the number of monikers we have given the penis. Here is a partial list of the terms I've heard in my practice, in alphabetical order: apparatus, bat, battering ram, bone, cock, dick, dingaling, dong, engine, equipment, gadget, gladius (a Latin word, meaning sword; the vagina was called a sheath), goober, horn, instrument, johnson, john thomas, joint, jolly roger, machine, manhood, manroot, member, organ, pecker, peenie, pee pee, peter, pistol, pizzle, prick, putz, rod, roger, salami, schlong, schmuck, shaft, thing, third leg, tool, wang, weapon, wee wee, weiner, wick, works, yard, zapper. And there are probably many more being invented every day by the younger generation.

Of course, individual men—or sometimes their lovers—tag their penises with affectionate nicknames. I had a patient whose wife called his penis Helmut because its head, the glans, reminded her of a helmet. A college friend called his penis Winchester, after the rifle. When flower power came into vogue, he dropped that aggressive image in favor of Mellow Yellow. Famous men with personal penis nicknames include Robin Williams, who used to refer to Mr. Happy in his stand-up routines; Lyndon Johnson, who, true to form, called his Jumbo; and the King of Rock 'n' Roll, who referred to his favorite appendage as Little Elvis.

The point is, in a man's psyche, the penis is king. The penis rules its owner like a king governs his citizens. Sometimes, like a potentate who obeys the will of his people, it does a man's bidding; other times it dictates its own terms and its own rules, which we don't always comprehend. Like a monarch, it sometimes acts in unpredictable, enigmatic ways; it can be despotic, capricious, and selfish, and at other times benevolent, magnanimous, and wise. When king penis issues a command, men have little power to disobey. It can turn the mind, the emotions, and the senses into obedient serfs.

This correlation between the dictates of the penis and how men behave—not just sexually but in general—can't be emphasized enough. My father used to say, "When it's soft I'm hard, and when it's hard I'm soft." If you want something from a man, the worst time to ask is when he is frustrated sexually. Far better to ask when he is sexually aroused and his blood has rushed to his loins, along with his willpower; chances are, he will sell his soul for satisfaction. The best time, however, is just after he has had a satisfying orgasm, when he becomes as soft as his sated member.

On a more abstract level, there is a powerful correlation between how men perceive their penises and how they perceive themselves. I have found that men who like their penises tend to like themselves. Men who trust their penises and have confidence in them also have trust and confidence in themselves. By the same token, men who distrust or resent their penises and are insecure about its size or ability to perform tend to have poor self-esteem as a whole. I can't tell you which comes first, the self-image or the penis-image, any more than I can solve the conundrum of the chicken and the egg. But I can tell you with confidence that it works both ways: a man who is unsure of himself sexually, or has an embarrassing sexual experience—say, premature ejaculation or failure to get an erection—will be shadowed in other aspects of his life by insecurity and self-doubt; and a man whose self-regard takes a blow in business will carry that into the bedroom because the penis embodies his sense of who he is. Naturally, this can work in a positive way as well: if a man satisfies himself and his partner, the next morning he'll approach his work with self-assurance; and, if he comes home with the esteem of his colleagues and the memory of a job well done, he is much more likely to glide boldly and energetically into the boudoir.

The penis is an extension of the ego and at the same time it shapes the ego. The penis receives its marching orders from the mind and at the same time it dictates to it. This basic truth of man's existence deserves to be brought out into the open and celebrated. Instead, we either deny it or act as if it were a curse inflicted on us by the devil.

WE ARE TRAGICALLY ILL-INFORMED ABOUT THE PENIS

To a large extent, the genitals (and male sexuality in general) are still taboo subjects. In an age when nude pictures are as easy to find as photographs of world leaders, and seminude bodies can be seen gyrating with a flick of a remote control button, the penis remains closeted behind a curtain of prudishness. Thanks to the candor of the women's movement and the social importance of childbearing, we are relatively well informed about women's sexuality and the anatomy of the female reproductive system. But when it comes to the penis and its attendant components, we are mired in ignorance. It constantly amazes me how little my patients know about their own penises— not just male physiology but what I call the penis mystique. Middle-aged men are constantly asking me questions that they should have been able to answer as teenagers. Worse, they are not only underinformed, they are *misinformed*. The myths about the penis are mind-boggling.

It's no wonder. The genitals are not only the most seldom viewed of our external organs, hidden as they are behind garments, but they are seldom even mentioned in man-to-man conversation, except when guys tell jokes or brag—and neither joking nor bragging is amenable to the spread of accurate information. The only time the penis is mentioned in classrooms is in attenuated descriptions of how conception takes place. In that context, that mysterious and magnificent organ is reduced to the status of a seed-planter. Most fathers are not much help either. They broach the subject only when forced to go through the obligatory facts-of-life ritual, which they rush through as if they can't wait to change the subject to baseball. And the information fathers impart to their sons can usually be summed up in the old *Hill Street Blues* line: "Be careful out there."

Men don't even get much help from their doctors. Pediatricians discuss the penis with adolescents only if they observe a physical anomaly or feel obliged to warn about pregnancy or sexually transmitted diseases. Nowhere along the line can a young man learn the biological facts, let alone fathom his mental and emotional relationship to his penis. And it doesn't get much better for adults. Doctors talk about the penis only when a patient brings it up because he has a problem. Even in the context of a general physical exam the physician will at most take a cursory look at the genitals for signs of gross abnormalities, and, in older men, examine the prostate gland. There might be an item on a questionnaire asking the patient if he's having problems with his sex drive, but that is hardly a suitable entry point for a fruitful discussion.

One reason for all this is our prim puritanical heritage. The very word "penis" still has a peculiar shock value. When many people hear it, they giggle or blush or avert their eyes. Indeed, when I was considering *Penis Power* as a title for this book, I was advised by patients in the communications industry that just having the word on the cover would be unacceptable to many booksellers. Certainly, the word perks up people's ears and puts many men on guard, even in a doctor's office.

The other reason men remain in ignorance of the penis is that most physicians are undereducated about it. Sure, as with every other organ, we are taught its basic anatomy and the biochemistry of what takes place when the penis does what it does (to the extent those subjects are understood at all). But doctors are taught precious little about the penis mystique, that curious realm where biology meets the mind and emotions: what makes the penis work and what makes it *not* work; why it seems to have a mind of its own; why it gets hard sometimes and not others; why some sexual experiences are more satisfying than others even though the exact same reflex action occurs with every orgasm; what is normal and what is not. These are the things that men wonder about but are embarrassed to inquire about. And if they *do* ask their doctors, they usually get inadequate answers. We do not know enough about these things scientifically, and the realm of the psyche is ignored in medical education, except in psychiatry classes, where the discussion is confined to pathology. If you can't ask your doctor, who can you ask?

Sadly, men get their most influential penis education from street corner and locker room banter, pornography, hot novels, and the images broadcast on the screens of the mass media. That education is a travesty. Knowledge of the penis is so central to a man's life, it is so natural, so normal, so vital, that it must be brought out of the closet into the light of day. Otherwise, the other trend I have observed—an epidemic of self-doubt and insecurity—will continue to grow.

AN EPIDEMIC OF PENIS WEAKNESS

This is one of the best-kept secrets in America. If my experience as a busy urologist is an accurate gauge, the last ten years have seen a dramatic rise in both real sexual dysfunction and imagined inadequacy. In fact, there is far more of the imagined variety: huge numbers of men *think* they are deficient in some way, or *assume* there is something wrong with them, or *fear* they are abnormal. Some come to see me specifically to talk about their sexual concerns. However, most of my patients come because of other urologic problems—kidney or bladder disorders, prostate conditions, and so forth—but they find a way to bring up their penis anxieties. For example, they might have a minor complaint such as a blemish, an irritation, an itch, or a burning sensation when they urinate, but they also have something else on their minds. I can almost predict the moment—as they are putting on their pants or reaching for the doorknob—that they will say, "By the way, Doc..." and then reveal their true concern, as if it were a mere afterthought.

What are they concerned about? It comes down to two categories: size and performance. With all due respect to Freud, in my experience, women do not have penis envy, they have penis curiosity. It's *men* who have penis envy. "Is it normal size, Doc?" they wonder. "Shouldn't it be bigger?" Some even ask if I have a way to make it longer or wider. We'll return to the question of size in a later chapter. The more frequent questions are actually about performance. These come in three varieties: sex drive, erections, and ejaculation.

Older men worry because they seem to have lost their libido. Middle-aged men are upset because they used to desire sex as often as they could get it but now make love only a few times a month. Even young men are occasionally concerned about their sex drive: "My friends are horny all the time. It's all they think about. Is there something wrong with me?" Then there are erection worries: "I can't get one"; "It takes me longer to get hard than it used to"; "I can't get it up more than once a night now"; "I lost it right in the middle of foreplay!" And, of course, there is ejaculation distress: "I can't come anymore"; "I used to have a big payload, now it's just a little squirt"; "My wife complains it takes me forever"; and the biggest panic-inducer of all, "My girlfriend says I come too fast."

Naturally, some of the questions my patients raise reflect serious medical conditions, and wherever that is even a remote possibility I treat it as such. A small percentage of sexual dysfunction complaints are caused by bona fide medical problems. Most of these come from older men with organic disorders that impede ability to achieve an erection adequate for penetration (the classic definition of impotence). A number of physiological conditions can cause impotence, including arteriosclerosis, diabetes, hormonal disorders, injuries, multiple sclerosis, reactions to medication, and substance abuse. We have made tremendous advances in the science of diagnosis and treatment. Sophisticated tests can now determine the exact cause of the problem or, equally important, rule out physical causes entirely. We also have a varied repertoire of excellent treatments for physical penis weakness. All of this will be described in a later chapter. Here it is enough to say that only a small percentage of patients who complain about their penises have genuine medical conditions.

The overwhelming majority of complaints I hear daily are expressions of insecurity, with no medical basis whatsoever. They are variations on one fundamental anxiety: "Am I normal, Doc? Am I okay?" In most cases my answer is, unequivocally, "Yes."

I tell my patients that penis power is 1 percent between the legs and 99 percent between the ears. The actual percentages may be off by a few points, of course, but I stand by the spirit of my words: the vast majority of men have perfectly normal apparatus. There is nothing wrong with them physically or anatomically. Whatever problem they have, or *think* they have, originates in their minds, even if it expresses itself in a penis that refuses to obey orders. Some men have chronic sexual dysfunctions that are cause for serious concern because they affect not only their personal satisfaction and their self-images but their marriages and the happiness of their partners. When these problems are rooted in deep psychological conditions, whether depression, childhood sexual abuse, or some debilitating inner conflict, they are best served by a qualified psychiatrist or psychotherapist. However, in my experience such cases are the exceptions. Most men can be helped with a simple change of circumstances or attitudes. But by far, most men who worry about their penises are perturbed because of the erroneous notion that they don't measure up to some mythological standard.

The problem is, when it comes to sexuality, ignorance can be as disastrous as it is in war. The nature of the brain-penis axis is so delicate that a lack of confidence or a fear of failure can easily become a self-fulfilling prophecy. If you think you're abnormal, if you're anxious about performing adequately, if you're afraid that your partner might be disappointed, then chances are you have already worried yourself into the very problems you fear.

Self-doubt is your penis's biggest enemy! It's a vicious cycle: doubt leads to penis weakness, then the bad experience increases the self-doubt, which means that the next time you have sex your anxiety level will be even higher, so the chances of the problem repeating itself are greater, and so on.

I assure you that the vast majority of men who complain of penis problems are either perfectly normal and don't realize it or are creating their own difficulties by walking blindly in the quicksand of doubt. It is amazing how much an injection of simple education and a strong dose of reassurance can do for them—just as you will be amazed how much the forthcoming chapters do for you, as we demystify the penis and examine all the factors that can render it weak.

WHY THE EPIDEMIC NOW?

Each individual case must be evaluated independently, of course, and I will discuss the major causes of penis weakness in later chapters. Here it is worth contemplating the social conditions that have created this scourge. It could be argued that it has always been this way, or maybe even worse, and that I have seen more penis weakness in the last ten years only because men today feel more comfortable talking about it. In my opinion this is not the case. There are powerful social and historical factors at work.

One factor is the increased stress level of society as a whole. Men who work long hours without enough sleep, exercise, or relaxation are often psychologically drained and physically exhausted when they get home. Add to that the usual suspects—financial anxiety, time pressure caused by rapid-fire pace of events, traffic jams, hassles with bosses, co-workers, or clients, problems with the kids, and all the other annoyances of contemporary life—and you have a picture of conditions that are not conducive to maximum sexual performance. This is compounded by the media's highly romanticized image of marriage and family life, which creates impossible expectations. It is difficult to be at your best at anything, especially sex, when you feel out of sorts physically or your mind is someplace else, preoccupied by problems. Few things have a more chilling effect on sex than anxiety. And tension exacts a heavy toll on an intimate relationship; it pollutes the atmosphere and fills the bedroom with emotional toxins.

Plus, stress has definite medical consequences that work against normal sexual functioning. During the stress response, blood is shunted away from the genitals to supply the large muscle groups of the arms and legs. Also, anxiety—including performance anxiety—increases the activity of the sympathetic nervous system and boosts the flow of norepinephrine, which constricts blood vessels. As we will see, this is precisely the opposite of what is needed for an erection, namely a smooth flow of blood to the penis.

The problem is often compounded when men use alcohol and drugs in an attempt to cope with stress. As Shakespeare observed, alcohol "provokes the desire, but it takes away the performance." The same is true of drugs, including nicotine and many prescription medications. For reasons I will explain in a later chapter, *the drugging of the American male is a major factor in the decline of penis power*.

The women's movement, for all its welcome advances, has inadvertently contributed to the problem. Once upon a time, a man's principal concern—in fact, usually his *only* concern—when making love was his own satisfaction. His efforts were devoted exclusively to obtaining an orgasm. The only thought he gave to performance had to do with seducing a woman into bed and getting an erection hard enough to penetrate. Having achieved those two aims, the pressure was off. It was smooth sailing the rest of the way; he could just let nature take over. Then society discovered the female orgasm. Women declared they too have a right to a climax. Now it might still be smooth sailing, but it's an obstacle course, in which men score points for technique as well as getting to the finish line. The goal is no longer just to ejaculate, but to satisfy your partner. And, in many minds, the man has a responsibility not just to bring a woman to orgasm but to multiple, ecstatic, earth-shaking orgasms. Now, that's pressure!

Needless to say, women have as much right to sexual satisfaction as men. And as I shall discuss later, it behooves every man to cater to his partner's pleasure if for no other reason than to enhance his own. But it is also true that both genders have been insensitive to the high level of *performance anxiety* brought on by the new rules. The situation is made even more complicated by widespread ignorance regarding female orgasm and the enormous range of variation in female sexuality. Millions of relationships turn into no-win situations when couples aim for some imaginary standard of satisfaction instead of attending to the nuances and preferences of the individual woman. From my clinical observations, the single biggest sexual worry of contemporary men is that they won't provide their partners with orgasms of spectacular quantity and quality. And if a man has even one humiliating encounter with a dissatisfied woman, he can succumb to that vicious cycle that begins in self-doubt and ends in actual penis failure.

This has been even further complicated by the widespread use of vibrators and other so-called sensual aids. I have had women patients whose use of vibrators has irritated their urinary tracts. I ask why they continue to use them. Typically, they reply that it gives them a level of sexual excitement they never obtain with their husbands or boyfriends. I even have patients who become so dependent on their vibrators that they stop having sex with men altogether. Of course, no vibrator has lips, hands, or a tongue, and no vibrator is programmed to hug you when you need to be hugged. But how can a human penis measure up to an inanimate object that is always hard, always ready to go, never asks for anything in return, and can be totally controlled? What penis could possibly move like a battery-powered, buzzing vibrator? This might be a minor factor in male insecurity today, but it is not to be overlooked. My hope is that so many men will read this book and elevate their sex lives to superpotency that vibrators will go the way of chastity belts.

In my view, perhaps the main reason for the increase in penis weakness is the way in which men learn about sex. Part of it is due to a simple lack of accurate information. For instance, a teenager came to see me about a minor abrasion on his penis. As I examined him and prescribed a medication, I could tell that he wanted to say something. Sure enough, he screwed up his courage and told me that he had sex with a girl the previous weekend and could not ejaculate. He was scared to death. Was there something drastically wrong with him? I asked when his most recent sex had been prior to that experience. About a week earlier, he told me. I asked if he masturbated often. When he got over his initial embarrassment, he admitted that he had treated himself to a veritable orgy of masturbation the day of his embarrassing experience. When I told him that anyone who ejaculates six times in an afternoon might have trouble doing it again two hours later, he was so relieved I thought he would kiss me.

Had this boy not had the nerve to ask, he might have carried the false feeling of inadequacy into subsequent sexual encounters and gotten stuck in a downward spiral of self-doubt. This happens tragically often to young men, especially around the issues of lost erections and premature ejaculation. They don't know that such events are common among their peers, that they happen at some point to every nervous young man. But because they are too self-conscious to mention the subject, they assume there is something wrong with them. In many cases they remain inhibited for years, if not decades, either avoiding sex or approaching new experiences with apprehension.

This is more true in the last twenty years than ever before because there has been so much more casual sex, notwithstanding the AIDS epidemic. Disappointments due to anxiety are far more likely when a young couple hop into the sack without the old-fashioned waiting period in which to develop trust and affection. Not that I advocate the old ways. I think casual sex can be terrific when people are knowledgeable, careful, and self-assured. But when the participants are nervous, awkward, and unfamiliar with each other it can sometimes be traumatic, and a few early traumas can scar a young man for a long time.

Unfortunately, the natural bravado of men runs counter to the need for accurate information. Teenagers are not likely to hear in the locker room or school cafeteria comments like, "Hey, guys, I was making out with Suzie and I came in my pants before I even had her blouse off" or "Man, I was just about to do the deed when my dick just folded up like an umbrella." Not even best friends confess such humiliations to each other, although they occur every weekend all over the world. Worse, what an adolescent boy *is* likely to hear are wildly exaggerated or totally imaginary tales of other guys' sexual exploits, and those become the standards by which he measures himself.

It doesn't get much better once men reach adulthood; there is just as much macho posturing in bars, golf courses, bleachers, factories, and offices as there is in malls and school-yards. The result is the widespread myth that a real man is ready to get it on anytime, anyplace, knows everything there is to know about sex and women, never doubts his virility for a minute, is never nervous or scared, and can satisfy without fail any woman who is willing. We don't see the real face of male sexuality, we see the mask. Which is why, in my experience, most men secretly believe that others enjoy sex more than they do, and what's more, that others are a whole lot better at it. It would be the same with athletic ability if you couldn't actually *see* your peers on the playing field.

Not only is self-doubt brought on by misinformation and lack of proper penis education, it is magnified by the mass media's obsession with sleek, young, perfectly proportioned bodies. Feminists have made us aware of how insecure women can be when they don't measure up to the idealized images in movies, commercials, and magazines. Well, it affects men too. Those handsome hunks with rippling stomachs and perfect pecs that parade before our eyes present an ideal of masculinity that few men can live up to, especially as they age. It's not just feeling that you won't attract the gorgeous models in the beer commercials, it's what those widely promoted standards of youthful virility do to a man's body image as a whole. You look in the mirror and see something less than what you see on TV or in a magazine and it chips away at your self-image. You think what you see in the mirror is inferior, even abnormal, when in fact what's abnormal are those images on TV. This is not just about vanity, it's about sex, because those images represent idealized sex objects. They are society's model of masculinity, and for men the concept of masculinity has more to do with sex than anything else because being a man means being potent and virile. Hence, each little dent in your masculine self-image adds to the sum of doubt that you carry with you to the bedroom. Your penis is part of your body, and your image of your penis, your perception of it, your attitude toward it—and therefore your sense of yourself as a sexual being—are linked to how you view your body in general.

Another media-related factor, perhaps an even bigger one, is the idealized image of the sex act itself. Sex is one of the few activities in life that we don't learn about by watching other people actually do it. Not *real* people at any rate. We can peek through the keyhole of porn films and, a bit more discreetly, mainstream movies, and with the aid of our imaginations we can spy on couples in the pages of books. This is hardly an education in realism. If a man's primary sources of sex information are movies and books, he can't help but get the impression that "real men" have huge penises that become hard as stone on a moment's notice and stay that way, throbbing and thrusting, plunging and pounding, until he and his lover—who is, of course, young, gorgeous, perfectly proportioned, and insatiable, just like the girl next door—reach, with the perfect timing of synchronized swimmers, a simultaneous, earth-stopping, shrieking orgasm.

When was the last time you saw, on screen or page, ordinary, run-of-the-mill sex? I assure you that what you commonly experience in the privacy of your bedroom is much more typical than the media fantasy model. Even if you had the help of Hollywood scriptwriters, directors, set designers, and special effects wizards, even if the London Symphony Orchestra accompanied your tryst, you would rarely duplicate what novels and movies tell us sex is supposed to be like. And what happens when reality does not measure up to the imagined ideal? Men blame themselves. They assume there is something wrong with them. They think they are failures. And what is the focal point of their disappointment? Their penis, of course. What's wrong with it? Why can't it be bigger and harder? Why doesn't it do what the throbbing ramrods in books do?

You might not hear men ask those questions, but I do, almost every day. Men think they should have a two-foot-long shaft of solid steel between their legs that can pump and pound for hours on end. That's not a penis, it's a pneumatic drill.

The bottom line is, most men measure themselves against standards built on fantasy, not reality. They interpret normal, commonplace experiences as signs of personal failure. In fact, there is enormous variety among men with respect to sex drive, capacity, preferences, standards of satisfaction, and so on. Yet they assume that there is something called "normal." They worry that every little sexual idiosyncracy they have is a sign of abnormality. Worse, if things don't go as desired, if they have a disappointing or embarrassing experience, they panic. As we've seen, they end up with self-doubt, and self-doubt creates fear, anxiety, and inhibition, which are bigger obstacles to sexual happiness than a construction crew in your bedroom.

The truth is, every man I've ever known has, at one time or another, lost an erection or ejaculated sooner than he would like. Every man is, at times, not interested in sex. Every man has failed to satisfy a partner. The ones who take such events in stride, knowing that they are perfectly normal, and march without hesitation to their next sexual encounter, are the men who have what I call penis power.

A WAKE-UP CALL

The sad part of all this is that millions of men—as well as their partners, of course—are being deprived of full sexual satisfaction. Nothing is more wonderful than the free and uninhibited expression of sexuality. Nothing is more glorious than the joyful sharing of physical pleasure between two generous, enthusiastic human beings. But judging from my experience, this plague of confusion and self-consciousness has caused most men to have less sex than they would like and to enjoy the sex they *do* have a lot less than they should. Sex should be fun, not a chore. It is life's cheapest luxury. But for too many men it has become a worrisome task, a source of tension, a burden, like a problem to solve or a test they have to take, when it should be a simple, natural pleasure that *erases* worries, tensions, and burdens.

As the product of the best medical education our country can offer and a urologist with a prominent, busy practice, I want to drive home the message that using your penis for the purpose nature intended is not only one of life's great pleasures, but also good for your health in general. It is good for your mood and your outlook on life; it is a natural tranquilizer with no bad side effects. Men who are frustrated sexually tend to be tense and irritable; they often seem angry at the world. Men who are sexually satisfied and feel good about themselves as sexual beings tend to have a positive outlook and a warm glow of health. Also, as a purely physical exercise, sex can't be recommended highly enough. It is excellent for cardiovascular fitness, it benefits circulation, it stimulates the nervous system and the prostate gland, it clears up mental cobwebs and invigorates the whole body. And contrary to certain myths, you can't wear out your penis with sexual activity, nor can you somehow use up your allotment of orgasms. As a man of science, I will sum up my judgment on the vigorous exercise of the penis with the childhood ditty that goes, "Use it, use it, you can't abuse it, and if you don't, you're gonna lose it."

Naturally, as a physician who has treated countless AIDS patients and seen many of them die, I would be the last person to advise anyone to turn back the clock to a less-troubled time. It *is* dangerous out there. However, there is no reason that this tragic epidemic should inhibit responsible adults who are aware of the risks involved in various practices and understand what it means to use discernment and the necessary means of prevention. There will be more to say on this subject in later chapters.

The purpose of this book is to help men upgrade the quality of their lives by fully expressing their sexuality—not with esoteric sexual techniques or aphrodisiacs or new discoveries about erogenous zones, but through a very simple premise: becoming absolutely one hundred percent at ease with your penis. I want to eliminate self-doubt and inhibition. I want to destroy penis weakness in all its forms, whether it is chronic or occasional, actual or imagined. I want to demystify the penis, erase all the mythology that surrounds it, and empower men to enjoy every ounce of pleasure that their wonderful organ was intended to give. And I want to help women become experts in the care and nurture of the penises they look to for their own satisfaction.

The book will help you become superpotent. By that I do not mean what you might expect. I do not wish to turn you into some stereotypical stud. I do not define superpotency according to arbitrary standards of frequency, endurance, or technique. That would be self-defeating; it would intimidate men even more than they are already and *increase* self-doubt and penis weakness. By penis power I mean achieving maximum enjoyment and satisfaction—for both you and your partner—as determined by your own desires, standards, and tastes. It means harnessing the full power of your penis by treating it with all the respect and appreciation it deserves. I am convinced that this will do more for a man's self-esteem than a year's worth of weekend warrior workshops. And I believe it will do more for the sorry state of male-female relationships than all the talk shows on television.

The basic messages I want to convey are the same ones I give my patients:

- Your penis is as big as *you* think it is; if you think big, you are big.
- Your penis behaves the way you tell it to.
- You are as potent as you think you are.
- You are okay. Your penis is okay.

A small minority of you have medical conditions that impede the sexual functioning of your penis. It is important to be aware of these conditions, as well as other physical factors that can affect your penis, and we will cover everything you need to know about that in Chapters Six and Seven. But unless you are one of those exceptions, you do not need specialized medical care. You do not need intensive psychotherapy. You need facts, you need a basic course in Penis 101, you need a change in attitude, and perhaps some tips on how to improve your sexual functioning.

You will find all of that and more in the chapters that follow. By the time you finish the book you will have what you need to maximize your penis power and live the rest of your life as a superpotent man.

2
Penis
Personalities

I t has a mind of its own." I hear that constantly from my patients in reference to their penises. One of the reasons we're so fascinated by that "junior partner," as a lawyer patient of mine calls his, is that it does *seem* to think for itself. What other organ grows to several times its normal size and then shrinks again, sometimes despite your intentions and without warning? What other organ behaves so capriciously and unpredictably? That's why we speak about it—maybe even speak *to* it—as if it were a person. Men say, "My penis did this or that" as if it makes its own decisions.

Of course, the reality is just the opposite. However much it appears to act of its own volition, your penis is not separate from yourself. It doesn't have a mind of its own; it reads your mind. Not only your mind but your heart and soul as well, for the penis is a direct reflection of who you are. It reflects your thoughts and your feelings more than any other part of your body. When you are up, so is your penis. When you are down, it will be down as well. When you feel strong, vigorous, creative, and confident, your penis is strong, vigorous, creative, and confident too. When you feel tired, apathetic, depressed, or impatient, your penis is tired, apathetic, depressed, or impatient.

The reason it *seems* to have a mind of its own and to sometimes act contrary to your wishes is because you are not always in touch with what you really think and feel. Your penis *is* in touch. It has a direct line to your brain. You can't fool it. If you're angry, nervous, or worried and try to hide your feelings by putting on a happy, sexy exterior, your penis will know the truth. If you're feeling horny but suppressing it for social reasons, your penis will know the truth. If your partner offends you or hurts you, you can bet that no matter how much you try to conceal your feelings your penis will act hurt or offended. If your partner adores you, flatters you, and wants you, your penis will respond accordingly, even if you don't think you're in the mood. In a sense, the behavior of your penis is a more accurate barometer of who you are at any particular moment than your own conscious assessment.

The behavior of your penis is an accurate reflection of your basic personality. Like the eyes, the penis is an organ of expression. It embodies your personality. That is why, over the many years that I have been examining penises and talking to the men they are attached to, I have observed a definite correlation between how men behave sexually and how they behave in general. Men with a negative penis-image tend to have a poor self-image overall, whereas men with a positive penis-image see themselves in a positive light. For the most part, we behave in the bedroom much the same way we behave in the living room, office, factory, freeway, or wherever.

In the rest of the chapter I will describe some of the basic penis personalities I've met in my twenty years of practicing urology. These are not mutually exclusive traits; any given man might partake of several of them, or shift from one to another depending on circumstances. You might want to see which ones fit you; and women might want to match the men they know to the personalities on the list.

Let's begin with positive penis personalities. These are traits worthy of admiration. Every man should aspire to these traits and do all he can to emulate them.

POSITIVE PENIS PERSONALITIES

THE PERCEPTIVE PENIS PERSONALITY

This is an understanding man with an understanding penis—one that can empathize with women in general and his partner in particular. He responds generously to his lover's needs and picks up intuitively on her unexpressed moods and desires. It is as if his penis were a periscope, poking its head above the surface into the light, where it can assess the psychological atmosphere.

THE PERSISTENT PENIS PERSONALITY

This man does not accept defeat. When he desires someone he pursues her with determination, not taking no for an answer until he is absolutely certain that "No!" is in fact what is meant. He pursues intelligently, diplomatically, and persuasively, not like a pest, a harasser, or a date rapist. And in bed he pursues the level of performance and fulfillment he and his partner desire.

THE PERCOLATING PENIS PERSONALITY

This guy is always cooking, always ready for action. Regardless of his age, he is dynamic, youthful, and energetic. He likes attention and seeks it out, but in a likable, endearing way, without arrogance or obnoxious bravado. I find that women like men with this personality. He's fun, he's exciting, and his percolating penis reheats quickly.

THE PENSIVE PENIS PERSONALITY

A cartoonist might picture this penis in a tweed condom and horn-rimmed glasses. He likes to think things through. He is intelligent, well informed, and clear-thinking about all things, which makes him a knowledgeable partner who tries to know as much as he can about sex and the woman he's with. He probes for fresh ways to bring pleasure to himself and his lover. One caveat, however: if this type gets *too* calculating he can miss out on a lot of fun because he's thinking when he ought to be feeling.

THE PHILANTHROPIC PENIS PERSONALITY

This good-hearted soul finds nothing more satisfying than giving pleasure to his partner. When not involved in a long-term relationship, he is drawn to lonely women in need of comfort or solace, or to romantic types who have been hurt by callous men and yearn for someone more generous and caring. He gives such women an emotionally rich sexual experience. But he has to be aware of one thing: being so concerned about his partner's fulfillment that he neglects his own needs and desires.

THE PEACEFUL PENIS PERSONALITY

A calm man whose penis is relaxed only in the psychological sense. It's in fact raring to go, but it comports itself with a cool, collected dignity. He is not complacent, nor is he apathetic or indifferent. He simply does not demand much and is able to extract great pleasure from whatever life places before him. He tends to be a gentle, tender lover, but highly passionate at the same time.

THE PIONEER PENIS PERSONALITY

Versatility is his name, imagination is his game. He is a trailblazer, willing to try anything new in the spirit of adventure and fun. He adapts to unexpected conditions easily and eagerly, whether an unforeseen tryst, a partner who is more voracious (or more reluctant) than he anticipated, or an unlikely location, whether the lavatory in an airplane or a broom closet. As one of my patients told me, "If oranges are in demand on Tuesday, you'd better have oranges for sale. If on Wednesday everyone wants bananas, you'd better get a truck-load of bananas." If you're a woman with esoteric inclinations or an attraction to new things, this is your guy.

THE PLAYFUL PENIS PERSONALITY

A party guy: upbeat, perky, maybe a little bit mischievous. He's full of surprises. He might swoop down on his lover when least expected or show up at her office and whisk her off to a hotel for the afternoon. If penises were automobiles, his would be a sports car. Always ready to laugh, he never takes himself or his penis too seriously. He might uncork a joke in the middle of making love and not miss a beat. To him, a woman with a sense of humor has the sex appeal of a centerfold, and his own funny bone is an erogenous zone.

THE PRECOCIOUS PENIS PERSONALITY

This is the young man who is sexually aware at an early age; he knows what to do and how to do it long before his peers. If he is mature enough to approach sex responsibly, he might be so active that it drives his buddies wild with envy. He doesn't have a shy bone in his body—or a shy *boner*. Older women might feel guilty about the feelings he arouses in them. It's not that he's necessarily good-looking; he just has that certain something that comes from penis confidence. And pre-cocity is not limited to the very young. A mature man can be a precocious penis personality in that he is up-front and very personal. He makes his intentions known, a trait that can be obnoxious in the wrong hands but charming in his. Women might be shocked for a moment, but they quickly recover and find him refreshingly direct.

THE PASSIONATE PENIS PERSONALITY

Rhett Butler and Prince Charming are his role models. He's a lover's lover, with boundless enthusiasm for life and love. Emotional, ardent, and lusty, he likes grand gestures and noble statements. He sends bouquets, he showers compliments, he spouts poetry, he dances cheek to cheek—and he always means it. He remembers birthdays and anniversaries, and if he forgets he'll make up for it magnificently. He is likely to have a clever nickname for his penis, something like Lancelot, and consider it a staunch friend and a trusted ally in the service of amour. Women find him irresistible. He's as sensitive as he is strong.

THE PRODIGIOUS PENIS PERSONALITY

His penis may or may not be prodigiously large, but he thinks and acts as if it is. This man not only has a bustling libido, he has an abundant heart and a generous soul. He sees himself as possessing great bounty, and he gives of himself freely, knowing that he will be replenished in return. He is ready for sex anytime, anyplace. A man of great penis largess, he is capable of extracting the maximum pleasure from any situation. Women are drawn to him, sometimes for reasons they can't explain. This is one sexy guy.

These positive penis personalities are all embodied in the ultimate penis personality: the superpotent man, whom I'll describe in the next chapter. First, let's look at what in my clinical judgment are negative penis personalities. These are to be avoided. If you possess some of these traits you will want to work at overcoming them, for they inhibit the full expression of your penis power.

NEGATIVE PENIS PERSONALITIES

THE PEEWEE PENIS PERSONALITY

This man thinks small. He perceives his penis as undersized and has an image of himself, psychologically, as a small man. He might try to overcompensate by being a shark in business or by driving fancy cars, but he views himself and his penis through the wrong end of a telescope. In reality, the odds that his penis is actually smaller than normal are astronomical.

THE PESSIMISTIC PENIS PERSONALITY

This guy is a downer, and his penis reflects that. He is a glass-is-half-empty sort of guy who approaches every activity feeling that it won't work out. This includes sex. Deep inside he feels that if he does manage to get a woman to bed his penis won't be big enough or hard enough, or he won't last long enough. Needless to say, his gloomy prognoses usually turn out right.

THE PETULANT PENIS PERSONALITY

Rude and insolent, this contentious guy wants to stick his penis where it's not wanted or is not ready to be received. He has to have things his way; if his partner hesitates to meet his demands, he acts as if he's being put upon. And if things don't work out it's always the other person's fault.

THE PROMISCUOUS PENIS PERSONALITY

He's always on the lookout for new conquests. Very insecure, he needs to carve notches on his belt, even if he's married. Needless to say, in the age of AIDS, this indiscriminate character is a dangerous man to get intimate with. I'm all for being sexually adventurous, and if variety is the spice of your life, more power to you. But I advise patients who, like an appliance, are ready to plug themselves into anything at any time that discernment will bring you less trouble and more pleasure in the long run.

THE PHOBIC PENIS PERSONALITY

Imagine a penis huddling fearfully inside a pair of pants and peeking through the zipper to make sure it's safe to come out. This personality has irrational aversions. Sexually speaking the phobia might be to certain smells, or pubic hair, or large breasts, or unlocked bedrooms, or the dark, or a hundred other things. He might be petrified of disease—not just worthy adversaries like HIV virus that causes AIDS but any conceivable germ in the environment. He might be terrified of vaginas, fearing that one will ensnare him like a Venus flytrap (this is not hyperbole; I have had a number of patients with that bizarre phobia). Any kind of irrational fear will keep a man from enjoying sex as surely as an acrophobe avoids tall buildings.

THE PICKY PENIS PERSONALITY

He is so obstinate and narrow-minded that he takes all the enjoyment out of using his penis. Everything has to be just so before he can function. His partner has to be this size and that shape, and do things his way, never mind what she likes. He's responsive only to a narrow range of turn-ons. When I see him as a patient, I find him pig-headed in the extreme. "Don't confuse me with the facts" is his attitude, even about his health.

THE PILE DRIVER PENIS PERSONALITY

This bulldozer approaches vaginas like a guy jackhammering cement in front of your house at 7:00 A.M. "Wham, bam, thank you ma'am" is an understatement. Crude and clumsy, he has no time for romance or foreplay. He pounds, plunges, and jabs, and sometimes actually injures his partners. This is not to say that he is vicious or sadistic. He might, in fact, be a pussycat. But when he's aroused, look out! If he's lucky he'll hook up with someone who enjoys this approach (and in my experience there is, indeed, someone for everyone), but any woman who finds herself with a pile driver is well advised to settle him down before she gets into bed, unless she enjoys feeling like a trampoline.

THE PERVERTED PENIS PERSONALITY

It is not my job to label any sexual act a perversion. In my experience, one person's perversion is another's pleasure, and as long as no one is being hurt or abused I have no philosophical or medical objection to any act between consenting adults. That said, I have observed a penis personality that is drawn only to acts that are on the edge. He's turned on by things that most people wince at and that his partner has to be seduced or coerced into joining. He reminds me of the wife in Woody Allen's *Everything You Always Wanted to Know About Sex (But Were Afraid to Ask)* who could have sex only in public places where there was a risk of being seen.

THE POMPOUS PENIS PERSONALITY

"Look at me. Ain't I something?" this type proclaims. I believe in penis pride; every man should have it. But this guy spills over into pure narcissism. He's the locker room braggart who spins crude tales about his conquests and prodigious feats. Even if his exploits are true, which is rare, his manner is so offensive that listeners conclude he's a phony. Just as it is unseemly for millionaires to boast about their wealth, men of true penis power don't brag about their sexual accomplishments. This arrogant, self-important type also misrepresents himself to women. He comes on like God's gift, promising a night of bliss, but he doesn't always come through. The penis is a great equalizer; it's the most honest part of a man's anatomy.

THE PROFESSIONAL PENIS PERSONALITY

Here we have the male prostitute and the gigolo, very unhealthy lifestyles to say the least, but interesting personalities. They are confident in their sexuality to the point of being cocky or arrogant, and they know how to exert their power. I also place the pimp in this category. I have treated a number of pimps over the years and found many of them fascinating even though their behavior is reprehensible. They have an uncanny ability to mesmerize women. Despite extreme mistreatment and exploitation, their women seem to enjoy bringing home money and having sex with them after a long night of servicing clients. Dealing with these men, I often find myself wishing that their positive penis attitude could be transmitted to men who would make better use of it.

THE PINCH HITTER PENIS PERSONALITY

What turns him on is clandestine sex with a woman who is cheating on her husband or lover. He's a stand-in, the guy who gets furtive phone calls and sexy invitations when the man in the starting lineup is out of town. Or he has short-lived affairs with women on the rebound who need companionship until the next real relationship comes along. He seldom has a satisfying long-term relationship, and while he might have fun when he's in the game, it gets lonely on the bench.

THE PIOUS PENIS PERSONALITY

He could be a minister, priest, rabbi, or mullah, or a devout layman assiduously trying to conform to scripture. In my clinical experience, men who abstain from sex because of religious beliefs tend to be torn by conflict. As a scientist, it is hard for me to comprehend how a man can restrain a normal sex drive without suffering debilitating consequences. Physiologically, they have the same needs as everyone else. Nevertheless, many pious men are able to keep their penises under wraps and maintain vows while exhibiting a sense of joy and a tolerance for those with more liberal attitudes. These men deserve and get my respect. But the man who struggles to repress his sexuality and resents having to bear that burden is to be pitied. And the pious hypocrite who cavorts with hookers while threatening "sinners" with fire and brimstone deserves neither respect nor pity.

THE PIPE DREAM PENIS PERSONALITY

Like a perpetual adolescent, he lives in a dream world where he is a combination of Sean Connery and Long Dong Silver, where flawless women lust for him and he satisfies their every desire. In reality, the only satisfactory sex he has is above the neck; his mind is X-rated, but his penis is strictly Family Channel. When I encounter such men I try to convince them to be proud of what God has endowed them with. If they use what they have intelligently and accept with gratitude the real sexual opportunities before them, they don't have to live for fantasies that will never come true.

THE PHARMACEUTICAL PENIS PERSONALITY

Some men need to medicate themselves before they can have satisfactory sex. Typically, that entails a few drinks, a tranquilizer, or a few tokes of marijuana to loosen their inhibitions. Others don't think they *need* drugs per se, but they prefer it; they turn to chemicals for heightened sensation, whether the drug of choice is cocaine, amphetamine, amyl nitrate, or whatever. This type is likely to become dependent on substances with harmful side effects. In the long term their penis power gets debilitated. I try to convince them that the benefits of drugs and alcohol are illusory and that they can function perfectly well without that assistance.

THE PISSED-OFF PENIS PERSONALITY

This guy is angry at the world, or maybe only half the world: women. He can't stand rejection, which he gets plenty of, and he can't stand honest emotions. When things go wrong it's everyone's fault but his own. Sexually, his hostility can express itself in a number of ways. He might satisfy himself without reciprocating for his partner; he might force his partner to do things she doesn't want to do; he might promise whatever it takes to get someone into bed, then flaunt his lies and leave; he might intentionally hurt his partner and act as though it were an accident. While in the context of a good relationship sex can be a terrific way to work off anger and frustration, I advise women to avoid men for whom sex is just an outlet for hostility.

THE PLAINTIFF PENIS PERSONALITY

A calculating type who adds up what he gets and what he gives and evaluates the totals according to his version of justice. I'm all for fair play when it comes to sex. However, the plaintiff personality has his own code and his own method of calculating. And when he comes up short he litigates: "I did this and that for you. Now you have to do X, Y, and Z for me." To my amazement, actual litigation can occur: one of my patients took his wife to court for denying him his right to more and better sex. She countersued, claiming that he had let himself go physically and was a chronic premature ejaculator.

THE PEDESTRIAN PENIS PERSONALITY

The missionary position is about it for him. He is unimaginative, mechanical, utterly without spontaneity—the sexual equivalent of an automatic camera that does everything it's programmed to do. A man of highly regimented routines, if his wife suggests catching a later train and grabbing a quickie in the kitchen, he thinks she's been reading too many romance novels. I try, usually in vain, to get these guys to loosen up.

THE POLITICAL PENIS PERSONALITY

A chameleon with an unerring knack for telling you what you want to hear, he alters his character to suit each potential constituent. But he seldom lives up to his campaign platform. If this type is in a position of power, he will not hesitate to use his status to service his penis, nor to use his penis to improve his position. If he could sleep his way to the top he'd be delighted, and if he can get a gullible, ambitious woman into the sack by promising her a seat on the fast track—or by threatening to demote her to the caboose—he won't hesitate for a second. To him, sexual harassment is just part of the law of the jungle.

THE POOPED PENIS PERSONALITY

Ho hum. This guy needs a long vacation. He's tired, burned-out, and limp, and so is his penis. More wives complain to me about this syndrome than anything else. Typically, the husbands are middle-aged, overworked, stressed-out professionals— lawyers, executives, even some of my medical colleagues. They work too many hours, shoulder too many burdens, and leave no time for the oldest and simplest form of rejuvenation. If there was a way to make love while mingling with movers and shakers, schmoozing a client, or closing a deal, they would do it more often, but by the time they get home to their spouses they can barely raise their fingers let alone their penises. I tell these men, "If you're too busy for sex you're way too busy."

THE PREOCCUPIED PENIS PERSONALITY

When the pooped personality isn't pooped he's preoccupied. This guy makes love on automatic pilot; his mind is always someplace other than where it belongs. It should be on his penis, his lips, his hands, or wherever on his lover's body they happen to be. Instead, his mind is at the office or the ball game and he's missing out on the best nontelevised sport in the world.

THE PARANOID PENIS PERSONALITY

This guy is so suspicious that if a woman is willing to go to bed with him he figures she's got ulterior motives. What does she *really* want? he wonders. If he can get over that hurdle, he'll worry about her father, her roommate, her ex-husband, her cat, or whatever strikes him as threatening. His lover can show him personalized data from the Centers for Disease Control and he'll still worry about the germs he might pick up from her. He thinks God made sexually transmitted diseases just to get him. Unfortunately, no one as fearful as this can live up to his sexual capacity.

THE PAMPERED PENIS PERSONALITY

This prima donna feels entitled to special treatment. You expect his penis to stand up and sing that song from *Funny Girl:* do for me, buy for me, lift me, carry me. Now, I believe the penis *should* be fussed over. It *should* be the center of attention. But demanding to be pampered without offering reciprocation or gratitude is not a sign of positive penis power.

THE PROCRASTINATING PENIS PERSONALITY

Why have sex here and now when you can put it off till tomorrow? That's the procrastinator. It's never the right time, place, or partner. If he wants someone he will put off contacting her for so long that she will probably forget who he is. The procrastinator is not lazy, he's scared. He's so terrified of penis failure that he can't bring himself to face the challenge.

THE PROFLIGATE PENIS PERSONALITY

There is no way you can wear out your penis by using it for its intended purpose. But you can damage other parts of your body by overindulging your penis. The profligate personality is given to dissipation. He is extravagant and wildly self-indulgent. Of course, those are relative terms: what is profligate for an older or ailing man might be harmless excitement for a young, healthy guy. But when you follow your penis to the point of not eating or sleeping properly, or jeopardizing your job or family, then you've gone over the edge.

THE POSSESSIVE PENIS PERSONALITY

"If you sleep with me, I own you." That's the attitude of the possessive personality. He doesn't want a lover, he wants a slave. Making some demands and insisting on fidelity are not signs of weakness. But this type wants to dominate and control his partner's life and every aspect of their sexuality.

THE PORNOGRAPHIC PENIS PERSONALITY

I have nothing against pornography if that's your taste. As a way of occasionally juicing up a relationship, it can be useful and it can be fun. But the pornographic penis *needs* erotic material to get aroused. To him, a warm body is not as stimulating as a moving picture or an erotic passage from a book. In general, my attitude is, whatever turns you on is okay, medically and ethically. But I always advise my patients to make the most of reality instead of relying too much on fantasy.

As I suggested earlier, reducing the number and intensity of these negative traits and emulating the positive attributes that began the chapter is the goal I would like men to shoot for. If you follow the advice in the rest of this book, that is precisely what you will achieve. But I have not yet described the ultimate aspiration, the penis personality that stands head and shoulders above the rest: the superpotent man. He deserves a chapter of his own.

3
The Superpotent Man

As a urologic surgeon, I have been privy to the intimate details of tens of thousands of patients' lives. In addition, other men—colleagues, friends, and family members—have taken advantage of my curiosity and professional status to discuss their sex lives. All this experience has enabled me to develop a portrait of a special penis personality: the superpotent man. As I describe his attributes, you might find yourself thinking, "I can't be like that. I'll never be that kind of guy." To which I say, nonsense! In fact, it is just those negative thoughts that prevent you from expressing all your penis power. In my view, superpotency is a birthright. It should be seen as the natural state of affairs, not the exception. Any man can achieve that power, and by the time you finish this book you should be well on your way to it. As you will see, superpotency is a consequence of positive thinking about yourself, your penis, and your sexuality.

Some men command attention. They fill the room. They turn heads. They are magnetic. Strong men view them with admiration and respect, while weaker men might be awestruck or intimidated. Women are stirred by such a man. They recognize his power, whether or not they are conscious of it. They tend to be attracted to him physically. If they are in the market for sex or romance, he's a top candidate. He inspires fantasies.

These men have a certain something. You might call it presence, you might call it sex appeal, you might just call it *it*. I call it penis power.

First, let me state unequivocally that penis power is not about looks or status. Superpotent men are not necessarily handsome in the classical sense. They don't have to be hunks. They wouldn't necessarily pass an audition for a beefcake calendar. They *might* be classically handsome, but it is not a prerequisite. There are handsome men with penis power and handsome men without it. There are homely men with penis power and homely men without it. Obviously, the guy who has both looks and superpotency has a lot going for him. But between a handsome man without it and a homely man who has it, it's the latter who will attract more women and lead a more satisfying life in general.

Look at certain movie stars who are considered sexy; some of them are not what you would call photogenic. Take the French actor Gerard Depardieu for example. He's a beefy guy with a big belly, a doughy face, and an oversized nose. Yet there is no denying his sex appeal. I don't know the man, but I'd wager he possesses ample penis power. Or look at Jack Nicholson. He's balding, potbellied, has weird eyebrows, and a face no Greek sculptor would use for a model. But he has something that women find irresistible. Then there's Carlo Ponti. Thirty years ago, the film producer was a small, bald, ordinary-looking man, the last man you would expect to see with a gorgeous, talented, voluptuous, sexy woman. But Ponti married perhaps the most desired woman in the world at that time, Sophia Loren, and he stayed married to her.

There are also plentiful examples of gorgeous hunks who satisfy every aesthetic criterion but don't arouse attention and are not necessarily sexy. I recall one day when an incredible physical specimen walked into my office. He was a professional athlete with a body of solid muscle and a face you would expect to see on a *GQ* cover. I assumed he was the kind of guy who had women falling at his feet, so I teased the secretaries, asking which one would like to meet him. No takers. "It's all on the outside," one of the women explained. "He just doesn't have it." The point is, superpotency is not about looks; any man who develops penis power will find that he looks better in his mind's eye and his physical attributes suddenly have more appeal.

Nor is it about wealth or social position. Superpotent men tend to be relatively successful in their chosen fields because their personal qualities foster achievement, but they are not all men of wealth and status. Sure, many women are attracted to men just because they are rich and powerful, but that appeal is often superficial and does not translate into true penis power. Once the fancy car is parked in its Beverly Hills garage and the two-thousand-dollar suit is hung in the closet and the silk underwear is removed, the rich man might be much less potent than the struggling artist in a garret or the assembly line worker in his tract house. Penis prosperity comes from within. The only form of abundance that really counts is an *attitude* of abundance, about oneself and one's sexuality.

I number among my patients and acquaintances some of the richest and most influential people in society. Many of them have abundant penis power, but some have power only in their offices and are plagued by penis weakness and personal insecurities. At the same time, I have known ordinary men who lead humble lives but are superpotent from head to toe. Penis power does not derive from mansions, yachts, and jewels. It derives from the heart and soul of a man. And it is far more valuable than the costliest luxury; it is, indeed, priceless.

Penis power is about *inner* qualities. What follows are the primary characteristics of superpotent men. They are within the reach of nearly every man. I suggest that as you read about them, you ask yourself to what extent you possess these traits. Where you find yourself lacking, make it a principal objective to develop those traits in yourself as part of your efforts to maximize your penis power.

THE SUPERPOTENT MAN EXUDES SELF-CONFIDENCE

This might be the most important attribute. To be a man of penis power you must believe in yourself. You must feel you can accomplish whatever you put your mind to. Superpotent men know who they are, accept who they are, and like who they are. They feel good about themselves and their place in the world. They have a certain contentment you don't see in men who are afflicted with self-doubt. At the same time, they don't rest on their laurels. They are curious about life. They love new challenges and new adventures, and they pursue their interests and ambitions with passion and conviction.

THE SUPERPOTENT MAN EXPRESSES HIS FULL POTENTIAL

I often ask men, "What are the things you've never done but want to do?" I've noticed that superpotent men often have to think before they answer. They might then mention a few items, but they do it with a distinct lack of concern, as opposed to the urgency and remorse expressed by men with major unfulfilled desires. Superpotent men don't wish they had done things other than what they *have* done. For the most part, they have achieved the goals they set for themselves at a particular stage of their lives because they live up to their potential in every respect.

This attitude was captured best by a colleague of mine, a fellow of enormous penis power in my estimation. We were riding up a ski lift early one morning when I asked him if there were things he had never done and wanted to do. The air was crystal clear and the sky the color of a blue jay. Bursts of golden sunlight danced on the white slopes. My friend surveyed the glorious scene as he reflected in silence. Finally, he said, "There are some things I'd still like to do. But if I were to die today, I would have no regrets." The point is, superpotent men succeed, just as the army recruiter lauds, in being all they can be.

THE SUPERPOTENT MAN HAS HEALTHY SELF-ESTEEM

Unlike men who *seem* to be self-assured but actually have fragile egos, superpotent men don't need constant reassurance from other people. They are secure within themselves. They don't have to go to great lengths to prove their worth or exhibit their penis power. They are proud, but they are not narcissistic or arrogant. This does not mean you have to blind yourself to your weaknesses. Men of penis power are secure enough to see themselves honestly, warts and all. If you have that kind of basic self-acceptance you can accommodate your human flaws and foibles without denial or overcompensation, and without succumbing to feelings of unworthiness.

THE SUPERPOTENT MAN IS A POSITIVE THINKER

Their glass is half full, not half empty. Every situation can be interpreted in a number of ways: you can choose to wade around in the murky waters of your mind or swim freely where the current of thought flows to a better place. This does not mean you should be a Pollyanna, putting a happy face on tragedies. It means not giving in to cynicism or despair. No matter what hand they are dealt, men with penis power accept it for what it is, find what is useful or hopeful in the situation, and take steps to turn it to their advantage. You must be bold in your aspirations and impatient with naysayers.

THE SUPERPOTENT MAN IS A WINNER

Put your heart and soul into all pursuits. Men with penis power tend to enjoy competition in a healthy way. They like coming in first, but they are good sports when they lose because they know they have done their best and their self-worth does not hinge on being number one every time out. They learn to take on challenges not just to achieve a goal but for the sheer exhilaration of the pursuit itself; a satisfying experience can be as important as a favorable outcome. All that matters is that they try their best. And when things go wrong, superpotent men bounce back quickly; they don't think of setbacks as failures. They assess their actions with honesty and clarity, learn from their mistakes, and pick up the pieces with fresh determination.

THE SUPERPOTENT MAN IS COURAGEOUS

The superpotent man is the guy you want on your side when the going gets tough. They are terrific under pressure. They keep their cool and they don't hesitate to take charge in a crisis. Whether or not you are a leader in the usual sense of the word is unimportant. You might not be in a position of authority, but if the going gets tough you want to be the one who knows how to transmute fear and tension into positive motivation and effective action.

THE SUPERPOTENT MAN IS EMOTIONALLY BALANCED

They have little anxiety and are rarely afflicted with nervousness or sleep problems. They are not prone to irrational fears or petty animosities, or burdened by feelings of guilt or shame. They seldom get depressed. Sure, if life throws a beanball at you, it's appropriate to get sad. It's okay to be vulnerable, and to be affected by loss and grief. But if you're a man of penis power you won't get down on yourself or grow bitter at the world, and you won't let yourself feel like a victim.

THE SUPERPOTENT MAN IS HAPPY

They enjoy life to the fullest. Whatever you do, wherever you are, be fully and totally there. Milk the present moment for all it's worth. Penis power usually translates to a good sense of humor. Not that you have to be funny or a sparkling wit. You might, in fact, be quiet and reserved. But the superpotent man has a certain twinkle that says, "I don't take myself or life too seriously." If you learn to appreciate the ironies and absurdities of life you can laugh just as exuberantly at your own foibles as you do at a good joke.

THE SUPERPOTENT MAN IS WELL-ROUNDED

Unlike one-dimensional men, they derive pleasure from all aspects of life, learning to approach every activity with a sense of excitement, enthusiasm, and appreciation.

THE SUPERPOTENT MAN HAS QUALITY RELATIONSHIPS

This goes for both their business and personal lives. Like all winners, men with penis power know that they *need* other people, whereas losers, as a psychiatrist friend once told me, *use* other people. In my experience, superpotent men treat people with respect and therefore command the same from others. Typically, they possess a certain charm and ease in social situations and are sensitive to the feelings of others.

These general qualities of superpotent men are all readily attainable if you adjust your beliefs and attitudes about yourself. Now let's look specifically at the attitudes and behavior of the superpotent man as they pertain to sex. As I said earlier, it is unclear what comes first, overall personality or penis traits, but I can state unequivocally, based on my clinical observations, that there is a powerful correlation between the two.

THE SUPERPOTENT MAN HAS A SYMBIOTIC RELATIONSHIP WITH HIS PENIS

You must view your penis as an integral part of yourself. In fact, in a certain sense, your penis is your most vital organ.

Not vital in the same sense that your heart and lungs and
kidneys are essential—that is, if they don't function properly
you die—but vital in the sense that your penis is the expression
of your spirit and individuality.

The superpotent man has a positive penis image to go
along with his positive image of himself as a person. He loves
his penis, respects it, and treats it well. He knows it can take
care of itself, so he never worries about it. Take pride in your
penis. It's your friend.

Let me distinguish the man of penis power from the others
who might *seem* to have those characteristics. The superpotent
man is not obsessed with his penis and he is not dominated by
it. Obsession is a sign of penis weakness. Let me put it this
way: if you meet a man who is obviously penis-obsessed, a guy
who is led around by his penis like a slave, he is most likely not
a superpotent man. He is probably disconnected from his penis
or in conflict with it. He is to be pitied, not admired. Men who
are really on top of their lives and their sexuality—men with
penis power—usually don't *seem* to be penis-oriented. Carry
your penis pride with dignity. You have nothing to prove, just
as you have nothing to hide.

It is also important to realize that superpotency has nothing to do with the size or appearance of your penis. The man of
penis power does not have some golden rod or magic wand
hanging between his legs. I can assure you as a urologist that
the penis of a superpotent man has no special attributes that
separate it from the penises of the rest of the species. The
differences are all in the mind—and heart.

THE SUPERPOTENT MAN HAS A HIGH LEVEL OF PENIS AWARENESS

He who knows himself understands his penis. Make an
effort to learn about the anatomy and physiology of the penis.
Get in touch with the likes and dislikes, quirks and foibles, of
your own individual penis. As your mind goes so goes your
penis. When you're tired or upset your penis will behave

differently from when you're energetic and upbeat. If you are angry at your partner your penis will express that feeling; if you adore your partner that too will be expressed by your emissary, Mr. Happy.

Penis awareness creates smooth, harmonious functioning between the mind and the penis. Generally speaking, the superpotent penis does what its owner expects it to do; it conducts itself in a manner consistent with how you want it to behave. Like a trustworthy business partner, it is far less likely to disappoint you or come up with unpleasant surprises.

THE SUPERPOTENT MAN HAS AN EXTREMELY SATISFYING SEX LIFE

If statistics were taken, superpotent men would be way above average in terms of frequency of sex and performance—not because they have gifted penises, but because they have a positive penis attitude. This will be true whether you are a single man with a variety of sex partners or a monogamous man with one partner for life. It will be true whether you are young and handsome or aging and ordinary.

However, it is important to note that penis power is not about performing Olympian sexual feats. Superpotent men do not necessarily go out and break records for frequency of intercourse or the number of orgasms their partners have or the number of times they can get it up in a night. Those are not the criteria of penis power. If they were, then the guys who perform in porno films would be the epitome of penis power because they can do incredible things, like get hard on command and ejaculate whenever the director orders it. But, in my opinion, porn stars are not men of penis power at all.

Don't measure your sexual self-worth by performance criteria. Any man whose self-image hinges on things like how often he scores and how great his performance is will probably *not* meet the standards of true penis power. To be a superpotent man, you must view sex as a pleasure, not a sporting event. It is not show business. You are not there to prove anything or to perform for anyone. You don't have to be what people would call a stud, and you certainly don't have to be a Don Juan or a braggart. What should matter to you is using your penis as often, and in such a manner, as is most satisfying to you and your partner. What you should really care about is that when you call upon your penis it functions according to your personal standards, not some imaginary yardstick. To be a man of penis power is to be content with yourself and your penis. That is the best and only criterion of satisfaction.

This is not to say that the penis of a superpotent man always performs to maximum capacity. It's just that it functions in harmony with the rest of him and its batting average is much higher than the penises of most men. When a man of penis power is let down by his penis, as happens on occasion, he takes it in stride. You should understand that such occurrences are to be expected from time to time, and the causes are circumstantial, not systemic. As a superpotent man, you can be a romantic and an idealist, but it's also wise to be realistic.

If you do have a disappointment don't view it as a disaster. Don't take it as a personal failure or a sign of pathology. Don't let it affect your confidence or self-image. What others see as a problem a man of penis power might see as a joke; he might find it terribly amusing that he and his penis are temporarily out of synch. Or he might see it as an opportunity because he is eager to face all penis challenges. Learn from your experience and move ahead, without hesitation or apprehension, to the next sexual opportunity.

THE SUPERPOTENT MAN IS AT EASE WITH HIS SEXUALITY

He loves sex, he thinks about it, it is important to him, he enjoys it to the fullest. But he doesn't make a big deal of it. In that respect, superpotency is like old money as opposed to nouveau riche. There is no need to be ostentatious or to call attention to yourself. In my experience, men of genuine talent and ability let their achievements speak for themselves, whereas men who find it necessary to boast are compensating for some perceived weakness. Men who talk about their sex lives a lot remind me of the target of the following joke. After examining a patient and listening to his extravagant boasts, a doctor tells him to give up half his sex life. "Which half?" asks his wife. "Talking about it or thinking about it?"

THE SUPERPOTENT MAN ENJOYS GIVING AND RECEIVING PLEASURE

In fact, he enjoys it immensely. That is the reason he has sex. Not only can you have it often but you can savor each and every experience. Take sex seriously, but not somberly. Be passionate and intense during sex—or frivolous, whimsical, and funny if the occasion calls for it. It's okay to laugh during sex, even at yourself. The superpotent man enjoys spontaneity and unpredictability, and he appreciates imaginative partners.

Most men of penis power have a wholesome appetite for new experiences. They thrive on variety, whether that means frequent encounters with an assortment of women or a wide spectrum of adventures with one. The penis power attitude is epitomized by the man who asked me a riddle: What is the difference between sex and wrestling? His answer: In wrestling, *some* holds are barred.

Speaking of variety, I must add that superpotent men are not womanizers in the pejorative sense of the word. Even those who eschew long-term relationships and move from bed to bed pursue their pleasure *responsibly*. Penis power, like all power, carries with it moral obligations; it can be used exploitively and abusively, or it can be applied with generosity and sensitivity. Superpotent men might enjoy sex whenever and wherever they find it, but they are not indiscriminately promiscuous. You don't have to pursue pleasure at the expense of a balanced life or other people's feelings. Your goal should be mutual enjoyment, not conquest.

Don't succumb to what is euphemistically labeled the "hard dick syndrome." The key is to keep your wits about you even when your penis is aroused and threatening to run amuk. Don't jeopardize important values for the sake of an orgasm. Be confident enough to know that there is always tomorrow— just like an experienced commuter doesn't risk his life by running wildly down the track to catch a train because he knows another will come shortly. Men of penis power are uninhibited and adventurous, but you must be aware of the ramifications of your actions.

Which brings up another trait, peculiar to recent times: *superpotent men do not take foolish risks*. As a urologist who has watched patients waste away and die of AIDS, I must urge you to educate yourself about sexually transmitted diseases and to value your life enough to exercise your penis power prudently. You need not be overly cautious, nor terrorized to the point of paranoia (something I have seen among many heterosexual men), but you must know the facts and how to enjoy an active sex life without fear. More on this important subject later. (See Chapter Eleven.)

THE SUPERPOTENT MAN LOVES WOMEN

They adore being with women. They love looking at women. They appreciate the feminine form in all its variety of shapes and sizes. The shape of a leg, the curve of a hip, the swelling arc of a bosom—the man of penis power savors these as nature's gifts. Is there anything wrong with that? Is it sexist? Is it exploitive? No; it's nature's way. Despite the rhetoric of extremists, most women understand that and appreciate it. That's why they wear short skirts and tight slacks, fuss with their hair and makeup, analyze the contours of their bust line and shop for bras with the most seductive lift. Women also do the same, i.e., they often like to look at attractive men and even mentally undress them. It is all part of nature's plan for keeping the species alive, and we ought to acknowledge it, celebrate it, and enjoy it. Let's take the guilt out of sexual attraction. And let's just accept the fact that men are voyeurs and sexual predators.

Having said that, let me make an important point:

superpotent men view women as sex objects, but not as *mere* sex objects. Let's be honest: women see men as sex objects too, and women like being sex objects to men. Problems arise when men treat women as if all they were good for was ogling or pawing or to provide a moist, warm place to put their penises. Problems arise when men fail to relate to women as complete human beings. Superpotent men do not have this problem. They appreciate all dimensions of a woman. They are capable of relating to women as equals. They have no need to feel superior. They are at ease in the company of women, and the feeling is mutual.

Sure, a superpotent man might pursue a liaison with persistence. But he does so with integrity, and he knows where to draw the line. He knows when no really means "No!" and when it means "Please try harder." They understand that rejection is a function of circumstances and individual taste, not a personal affront. Hence, they have no need to force themselves on anyone, and they have no desire to hurt anyone.

In a word, they have *judgment*. As a surgeon, I often say that you can teach a gorilla to do an appendectomy, but you can't teach a gorilla *when* to do one. That takes judgment, and in sexual behavior, as in surgery, judgment separates the men from the boys. Men of true penis power don't use lies or deception to manipulate women into bed, and they certainly don't use physical force. They don't play games that can cause anyone pain or anguish.

THE SUPERPOTENT MAN GIVES OPENLY AND WITHOUT RESERVATION

You should care about your partner's sexual pleasure as much as your own—not for the sake of macho pride and not because you are a self-sacrificing saint, but because you care about a woman's satisfaction and you know that the more you give the more you will get in return. Because it matters to them, superpotent men learn to be responsive to the needs and desires of their sexual partners. They also understand feelings and the importance of open and honest communication. Listen when a woman tells you she likes it when you do this to her vagina or that to her breast, and do your best to accommodate her preferences. Ditto your own. You should have no reservations about asking a woman to do the things that turn you on.

THE SUPERPOTENT MAN DOES NOT HAVE PERFORMANCE ANXIETY

This is perhaps the most salient distinction between men with penis power and men with penis weakness. Several studies have been done in which sex partners were observed in a very aroused state, usually brought on by the viewing of erotic movies. The men who had earlier stated that they functioned sexually in a satisfactory manner showed a marked increase in arousal after the erotic films. This was in sharp contrast with the men who admitted to some degree of sexual dysfunction. That group had a marked *decrease* in arousal after watching the movies. Why? Because as their partners became more responsive they started concentrating on *performance* concerns. They worried whether they would function okay, whereas the other, more confident men focused on the erotic cues of their aroused partners and got more turned on.

This is exactly why, as a superpotent man, you will be able to give your partner greater satisfaction. You will not be inhibited by self-doubt. You will respond to your partner's arousal with the full confidence that you will rise to the occasion. Stated another way, men of penis power develop a positive feedback loop. It starts with an aroused partner or an invitation to sex, which immediately registers a positive expectation of the forthcoming experience. You then make an accurate assessment of the sexual demand that is being made and focus on meeting that demand with a radarlike ability to tune in to your partner's cues. That is where your attention should be, not on your own performance. This leads automatically to greater penis arousal, which loops around to a heightened attention to sexual cues, which leads to greater arousal, and so forth, concluding with a mutually satisfying experience.

By contrast, a man of penis weakness has a negative feedback loop. A sexual proposition elicits a negative expectation, which leads to self-consciousness, which leads to an inability to perceive his partner's cues, which leads to decreased arousal, which confirms his negative expectation, increases his performance anxiety, impedes his ability to function, and leads to future avoidance.

To become a man of penis power, try to become a master of the positive sexual feedback loop.

THE SUPERPOTENT MAN KNOWS HOW TO HANDLE STRESS

This applies to all forms of stress; superpotent men do not succumb to anxiety or depression in any circumstances, above all sexual situations. Because they are adventurous, superpotent men run into situations that other men find inhibiting, such as an aggressive partner or a woman who prefers unusual sexual activities. To a man with penis weakness this might be a stressful situation eliciting fear and self-doubt. The superpotent man responds like an athlete up against a worthy opponent or teamed up with a great partner—it brings out the best in him. Your attitude should be, "My penis is my friend. What's good for him is good for me. He never lets me down." If you start to feel anxious, turn that feeling into positive energy; you can convert that anxious, edgy feeling into stimulation and become *more* aroused, not less.

Nothing is more debilitating to sexual satisfaction than anxiety and depression. Even though depression is known to diminish sexual desire and responsiveness, such a result is not inevitable by any means. The inevitable valleys in the contours of a man's life do not have to interfere with his sexuality. Even a superpotent man is vulnerable to the occasional "situational depression" and to the worries and fears that afflict all humans at one time or another. But if you have faith in yourself and

learn how to extract the positive elements from every experience, you will climb out of depressions quickly and convert
your worries into effective action. To become a man of penis
power you *have* to develop the capacity to not let negative
emotions impede your ability to achieve an erection. You must
not let the stress of your outside life intrude into the bedroom.
If you're a downer, rest assured that your penis will be a
downer too.

These are the chief characteristics I have observed in
superpotent men. But they are not all cut with the same cookie
cutter. There is a tremendous range of variation among men
with penis power. They are tall and short, plain and handsome,
young and old, rich and poor. Their penises are big, small, and
average. They have sex all the time, frequently, or only on
occasion. They are bold and aggressive or coy and self-effacing.
They like blondes, brunettes, or redheads, dark women or pale,
tall or short, buxom or slim. They prefer the missionary position,
or sitting up, or doggie style, or with the woman on top—or all
of the above. They like it in the morning, at night, in the
afternoon, or all times of the day. There are an infinite number of
ways to express penis power. Yours is as good as anyone else's.
The important thing is to have that power and embrace it.

Superpotency is within the reach of every man. It is not a
superhuman state; it is normal and natural, and you will be
surprised how easy it is to achieve. In my practice, I've seen
men become superpotent after learning a few facts and getting
a simple pep talk from me. They readjust their attitudes about
themselves and their penises and they're off and running.
Other men have to work at it for some time, or avail themselves of the specific procedures you will find in later chapters.
These tips helped them change their sexual behavior, which
gave them added penis power and served as proof, to themselves, that they were capable of being superpotent.

But the one thing that almost all men need is the penis
education they should have received when they came of age.
That is the purpose of the next few chapters.

4
The Staff
of Life

I t never ceases to amaze me what the average adult knows and mostly *doesn't* know about the penis. Most people have a pretty good idea of how the heart works, what the lungs and kidneys look like, what happens to food as it works its way through the digestive system, and even how babies are born. But half the human bodies in the world have this odd-looking appendage dangling from between their legs—an organ that we count on to propagate the species and provide one of the most sublime pleasures nature allows—and the average person hardly knows a thing about it. My patients, both men and women, ask so many elementary questions about the anatomy and functioning of the penis that I am often embarrassed for them.

The strange thing is, most people are extremely curious about the penis. They have been curious ever since they were old enough to notice that some kids have them and some don't. But this natural curiosity was suppressed. We were told it was improper to ask questions about the genitals, particularly the penis. We were told that our queries would be answered when we were older. But they seldom were, and most adults are too self-conscious to seek out the information on their own. So let me provide a concise layperson's guide to the concerns most people have about the penis.

LOOKS AREN'T EVERYTHING

It is, I must admit, an odd-looking organ, with its wrinkles and folds and wriggling network of red-and-blue pathways. Aesthetically speaking, most people, regardless of gender, do not find the penis terribly attractive. Some even find it curiously ugly. I am reminded of a remark made by the wife of a fellow urologist. We were talking one day about a case of hypospadias. This is a rare abnormality in which the urinary opening is not in its normal location at the tip of the penis but somewhere along the shaft instead. The deformity is often compounded by a fibrous band of tissue, called a chordee, which gives a peculiar downward curvature to the penis. I asked my colleague's wife if she knew what a hypospadias was. She replied, "Yes, that's a penis that's uglier than usual."

A very sophisticated woman who, by her own admission, had seen a significant number of penises prior to marrying a urologist, was saying, in effect, "The usual penis is also ugly." Unfortunately, that is a common point of view. Even if you were to eavesdrop on women's most intimate conversations, you would seldom hear them talk about what a gorgeous penis a man has. They talk about how handsome he is, they might praise his strong, muscular physique or sigh over his biceps, his legs, or his behind. But seldom will they single out his penis as being particularly attractive, just as men don't talk about beautiful vaginas the way they do breasts or legs or even hair. When women hoot and holler over male strippers at places like Chippendales, they are reacting to everything *but* the penis. They are turned on by the fabulous bodies of those gyrating hunks and the way the dancers tease them with their *unexposed* penises. The excitement comes from the *possibility* of exposure and from wondering what it looks like. But if a stripper were to actually bare his member, the thrill would quickly dissipate... unless there was a possibility that it would become erect.

This is a shame. As a urologist and a man, I wish the penis were viewed in a more positive light. There is no reason it shouldn't be. There is nothing intrinsically ugly about it, or about the vagina for that matter. The perception we have is, I believe, a cultural artifact with roots in the same tradition that holds sex—and therefore the organs that carry it out—to be dirty and debased. The penis should be viewed as beautiful. And if you can't find it in yourself to feel that way about *all* genitals, then at least see your own as beautiful—or if you are a woman, see your lover's that way. It is a question of attitude. Just as parents see their own children as beautiful regardless of how homely their actual features might be, so can we look at what has been considered a homely organ and find it lovely to behold.

Why does this matter? Because, just as children who are told they are beautiful think more highly of themselves, so would a man feel better about himself—and his sexuality—if he were told that his penis is beautiful. The more beauty a woman sees in her man's penis, the more *he* will like what he sees when he looks in the mirror. As a result, he will attribute more good qualities to his penis and bring more confidence to the bedroom. It's a question of positive reinforcement, and I can assure you most men need as much of it as they can get in regard to their blessed organ. There is no reason this can't be accomplished. We view all things in life through three eyes: the two flanking our noses that tell us grass is green and the sun is round; and the eye in our minds that sees with imagination and emotion. It is the mind's eye that can turn something with little inherent beauty into something glorious and unique.

Perhaps if the penis were less concealed, if it were more openly portrayed in art and film, it might come to be better appreciated as an object of aesthetic pleasure. For one thing, we would come to respect the vast range of differences among penises. In my twenty years in medicine, I have seen more male organs than you would see if you filled the Rose Bowl with naked men, and I can tell you without reservation that I have never seen any two that look quite alike. If nothing else, greater visibility might demystify the penis and make men less self-conscious about their own. And that, in turn, might raise substantially the overall level of penis power.

ONE SIZE FITS ALL

Of course, it is not so much the appearance of the penis that concerns men, but rather its size. I can't count the number of men who have asked me—as if it were just some casual question that happened to occur to them at that moment—if the size of their penis was "normal." Needless to say, they were not worried that it might be too big.

This preoccupation with penis size is one of the saddest and most ironic things I encounter as a urologist. Men compensate for their insecurity with humor. Hence, they probably tell more jokes about penis *size* than anything else, with the possible exception of wives. For example, one of the best tells of a man playing golf. He hits the ball into the rough, and while he is looking for it he sees a pair of tiny feet sticking out of some brambles. He pulls them and frees a leprechaun, who, in appreciation, grants him a wish. "I want the biggest dick you can give me," says the man. Well, he gets his wish, but his penis becomes so big it sticks out the bottom of his pants, drags on the ground and needs to be tucked into his socks. Overall, it becomes quite a nuisance.

The next time out on the links, the man meets the same leprechaun. "How's it going?" asks the wee one. The man explains his predicament, and the leprechaun, feeling compassionate, grants him another wish.

"Great," says the man. "Can you make my legs about four inches longer?"

That joke says everything you need to know about what penis size means deep within the minds of men. The *myth* that size is important is one of the cruelest hoaxes ever perpetrated on mankind. But it is so deeply imbedded in the collective consciousness that men are extremely sensitive about the length of their penises. Therefore, let me state unequivocally: there is nothing to worry about because one size fits all!

YOUR PENIS IS NOT TOO SMALL

I can state that with almost perfect certainty. I assure you, the variation in size among human penises is less than for hands, fingers, or noses. Statistically, penises can be as short as one and a half inches or as long as eight, but the number of organs that fall at the extremes are exceedingly few. The average length of a penis in its fully flaccid state is about four inches, and the overwhelming majority of men fall within centimeters of that average. Penis girth varies less, ranging between one to one and a half inches in diameter when flaccid.

A very tall man might have a longer penis than a very short man, just as he will probably have bigger feet and hands, but the difference in penis size between two such men will be *far less* than that of their other appendages. In other words, a short man's hand might be three full inches shorter than that of a tall man, he might wear a size eight shoe compared to a size thirteen, but his penis might only be a fraction of an inch shorter. In fact, I have often seen penises on short men that were as big, or bigger, than those of most basketball players.

Far more pertinent, given the concerns of most men, is the size of the *erect* penis. It averages about six inches long (although most of my patients prefer the term "half a foot long"). More important, the variation in size of the erect penis is far less than that of the flaccid penis. In other words, if one man's penis is five inches long when soft and another's is three inches long, that two-inch size difference is likely to shrink to near zero when they become erect. In fact, it is possible for the smaller penis to be bigger when erect.

The point is, the size range for erect penises is simply much less than that of flaccid penises. It is as if nature wanted so much for humans to propagate that she made it possible for just about any man, regardless of his overall size, to mate with any woman. So when you hear men brag that their penises are a foot long, take it with a few pounds of salt. They are either rare exceptions or liars (unless they are adding to their measurements that portion of the penis that we don't normally think about because it is inside the body; like a hose attached to a sink inside a house, the penis actually begins several inches deep in the abdominal cavity).

In fact, when people ask (as they do far more often than you can imagine) what is the biggest penis I've ever seen, I tell them it did not belong to any of the oversized professional athletes I've examined, or to any of the Hollywood studs. It belonged to a short, slightly built old man who was having prostate surgery. A pleasant, mild-mannered, pious man in his eighties, he was married to the same woman his whole adult life and neither one of them had the faintest idea of how relatively huge was the penis that had sired their nine children. I can tell you I've never had so many helpers in the operating room; half the nurses in the building wanted to assist just to check out the patient. The point is not that we're not *interested* in size, but that most wives and lovers don't care that much. Nurses might look in awe at a huge breast or foot too.

PENIS SIZE IS IN NO WAY RELATED TO PENIS POWER

Once I assure my patients that their penises are well within the normal range, I hammer home this crucial point: *superpotency has nothing to do with how big your penis is.* When a superpotent man makes love he is totally immersed in the erotic physical sensations and the emotional feelings of intimacy and tenderness. The last thing on his mind, or that of his lover, is the *size* of his penis. I have seen men with larger-than-average penises who are plagued by sexual dysfunction, and I have seen men with relatively small penises who represent the quintessence of superpotency.

In all my years of dealing with patients and their wives and lovers, I have never had a woman complain to me that her man's penis is too small. It is conceivable that some women make such complaints to their gynecologists or female physicians, but in my experience a prodigious penis is simply not a priority for the vast majority of women. Female colleagues with whom I've discussed the issue concur. A much more common complaint is that a lover's penis is *too big.* Intercourse can be painful for a woman whose vagina can't accommodate a large penis. I have actually had women ask me to surgically reduce the size of their husband's penis. There is no such procedure—just as there is no procedure to make them bigger. Penile prostheses, which are sometimes implanted surgically to treat organic impotence, do not enlarge the penis; they merely fill spaces in an organ whose size is determined by heredity.

The old homily, "It's not how big it is but how you use it," is one of those clichés that holds up to close scrutiny. Many of my women patients complain that their man doesn't get aroused often enough, that he's not imaginative enough, that his penis does not get *hard* enough, or that he doesn't last long enough during intercourse. But they never complain that his penis is not long enough or wide enough. To quote one female patient of mine, a true sage: "I don't care how long it is, I don't care how fat it is, I don't care how good-looking it is. I just care how *hard* it is!" Even more important, what women care about is not the size of your penis but the size of your heart and soul. They want a good, caring, responsive lover who is sensitive to their needs and desires.

True, many women discuss penis size lasciviously with their friends, and some will fantasize about men with enormous members. If they sleep with a man who is particularly well endowed, they might even *think* that they enjoyed it more. I attribute this to the power of imagination. We think bigger is better, and we associate the phallus symbolically with potency. Some women's fascination with large penises is not unlike a man's attraction to large breasts or a shapely behind. Finding someone with those features might enhance the sexual experience simply because it fulfills a fantasy, or because it is unusual, not because women with large breasts are better in bed or have more hospitable vaginas. Physiologically and anatomically, what occurs during intercourse has absolutely nothing to do with the size of any body part. The orgasm is exactly the same regardless of the physical features of the partner. What is different is entirely a product of emotions and imagination.

Certainly, a woman with an exceptionally large vagina and a man with a very small penis might be sexually incompatible due to the relative size of their genitals. But the possibility of a major mismatch is relatively remote. Lovers, like water, tend to seek their own levels. However, I do know of such a couple. The woman was nearly a foot taller than the man. They were hopelessly in love but dissatisfied sexually because, they believed, his penis was the wrong size for her vagina. But through experimentation they learned to adjust their positions and angles during intercourse and to vary their sexual practices so that eventually both were more than content.

There are sound physiological reasons why size doesn't contribute much to satisfaction. Nature, in its wisdom, has placed the principal nerve endings that produce sexual pleasure and orgasm right up front where they can be stimulated regardless of size. The man's are on the head of the penis, and the woman's are on the clitoris, within easy reach of any penis, small or large. In most positions, during penetration the thrusting movement of the penis inescapably brings it into contact with the nerves of the clitoris.

YOU'RE AS BIG AS YOU THINK YOU ARE

The only advantage a man with a large penis might have is if he *thinks* he has an advantage. So potent is the power of the mind to influence sexuality, and so strong is the myth of the importance of penis size, that if a man thinks he is exceptionally big he might start *acting* big. He might develop such a strong sense of confidence and penis pride early in life that this alone, not the actual size of his penis, might endow him with exceptional penis power.

Unfortunately, far more men think they are too small, and the exact opposite self-fulfilling prophecy takes place. It usually starts at puberty, when boys start to be self-conscious about everything associated with masculinity: Am I tall enough? Am I strong enough? Do I have pubic and underarm hair? Is my penis big enough? So insecure are most young boys that they magnify any sign of inadequacy they perceive. Foolishly, they compare themselves to older boys and men, or to peers who happen to mature faster, and they end up convinced that they don't measure up. They look down and see a puny, shriveled-up gherkin, then look across the locker room at someone else's dangling zucchini and they feel inferior.

It doesn't end in adolescence either. Sometimes it even gets worse, especially if they hang around with guys who brag—or, more likely, lie—about the size of their erections, or tell jokes that leave the impression that a small penis is tantamount to being effeminate. Watching pornographic movies makes things even worse. Whoever casts those films must scour the earth for men with exceptionally large members. Then they use all sorts of tricks with lighting and camera angles to make them look even bigger.

Many men feel worse about the size as they age because they think their penises are shrinking. What actually happens is they start to gain weight and the added layers of abdominal fat obscure the base of the penis, which used to be visible. This is why chubby men appear to have small penises—especially in their own eyes, looking down over a potbelly—and slim men appear to have big ones. In fact, there is no significant difference in size, especially when the penis is erect, but in the obese man it has to traverse two, three, or four inches of prepubic fat from under the pubic bone, where the base of the penis starts, until it is visible.

A man who does not learn the truth about penis size can be adversely affected by thinking his is too small. The sense of inadequacy can persist throughout his adult life and probably manifest as self-doubt about his penis behavior. He thinks he is inadequate anatomically, so he must be inadequate in performance as well; and, of course, that very inadequacy will then manifest in his behavior. Think small and you are small.

Fortunately, the corollary is equally true: *think big and you are big*. That is the most important thing for a man to know about size. What matters is the size of your self-esteem and the size of your heart, *not* the size of your penis. Besides, even if it did matter, there is absolutely nothing you can do about it. Size is strictly determined by heredity. You can pull on it day and night and it won't get longer. You could try hanging weights from it, like men in a certain tribe in Uganda, and you might succeed in stretching some ligaments to the point where it looks longer, but it won't be longer when it's erect anyway, so why take the risk of permanent injury? The best answer to the question "How big is your penis?" is a firm, unequivocal, "Plenty big enough!"

5
A Hard Man Is Good to Find

Like some two-headed Hindu god, the penis both creates life, by propelling semen toward fertilized ovaries, and preserves life, by expelling from the body toxic substances in the form of urine. Both responsibilities (which cannot take place at the same time, thanks to some very efficient engineering) are carried out through the urethra. Obviously, both functions of the penis are vital, but it is ironic to note that, medically speaking, if a man were, God forbid, to lose his penis he could still urinate and excrete nitrogenous waste, but he could no longer copulate.

Let me quickly dispel two misconceptions. One, the penis is not a muscle. There are no muscles in it, except for the smooth muscles of the blood vessels. Second, despite the colloquial term for erection, "boner," there are no bones in the penis. Beneath the skin—extremely sensitive skin, it should be noted, especially the part we call the head, or *glans*— the penis is composed of three cylinders made up of spongy tissue.

One of these cylinders is called the *corpus spongiosum*, which runs along the bottom of the penis and encircles the *urethra*. The urethra is a rather long canal that runs from the bladder all the way through the penis to the *meatus*, which is the hole (sometimes humorously referred to as the "eye") at the very tip of the organ. It is through the urethra and out the meatus that the penis delivers the goods in both its jobs, elimination and reproduction.

The other two cylinders run side by side along the upper part of the penis, consuming most of the space inside the organ. Called the *corpora cavernosa*, these tubular compartments consist of spongelike tissue filled with blood vessels and tiny chambers called *sinusoids*. If you were to look at these corpora through a microscope you would think you were seeing an aerial view of a delta, with rivers, tributaries, and pockets of ponds, marshes, and lakes. Each tube is surrounded by a tough fibrous sheath (*tunica*), which joins forces with the interior blood vessels to create erections. In fact, it is the absolute interior volume, limited by the rigid tunic, or coat, that dictates the size of an erect penis.

WHATEVER TURNS YOU ON

Erections are the result of a complex process involving the endocrine, muscular, vascular, and neurological systems—all of which are affected by psychological and emotional factors. We don't yet know all the intricate dynamics of *how* erections come and go, and we are especially in the dark about the all-important brain-penis axis, but we do understand many of the essentials. The penis gets hard in a series of distinct steps. The first occurs when the nerves are stimulated, causing microscopic blood vessels in the corpora to dilate. This is what we commonly call arousal. The factors that excite any given man at any particular time are enormously varied and idiosyncratic. As the pioneering sex researcher Alfred Kinsey wrote, "There is nothing more characteristic of the sexual response than the fact that it is not the same in any two individuals."

Whether the stimulation begins with something a man sees, hears, smells, feels, or imagines, it is the brain that determines the level of arousal. These complex neural connections between the brain and the penis are difficult to define and quantify, but the link is so intimate, immediate, and responsive it is as if the penis had senses of its own. Certainly it seems that way to an aroused man.

Obviously, the penis responds to *touch*. It is an exquisitely sensitive organ—the glans in particular, but also along the shaft. Exactly what kind of touch will arouse any particular penis is entirely a matter of individual preference, conditioning, and circumstances. Some men like a soft, gentle touch while others prefer a vigorous, perhaps even rough stroke; some men respond to the friction of a dry touch, while others favor it moist; some find slow, rhythmic movement a turn-on, while others go wild over rapid, irregular motion. And, of course, some like all of the above to different degrees at different times.

With the exception of men who have moral or religious objections, and those with an irrational phobia toward it, I have never met a man who did not respond to oral contact. It is not just the texture of the lips and tongue on the penis, and not just the psychological charge of having a woman perform such an intimate and generous act, it is the actual physical effect of sucking. Sucking creates a vacuum, a negative pressure within the corpora, which literally draws blood into the organ, and that blood flow is what brings about an erection.

Of course, the penis doesn't respond to touch only on itself. It perks up when other parts of the body are touched erotically: the thigh, the buttocks, the belly, the neck, the lips, and so forth. And, naturally, your penis can get aroused when you touch the right parts of someone else's body. Clearly, then, the penis's all-around sense of touch is vital in arousal.

The penis also has a sense of *smell* in a manner of speaking—just ask anyone in the perfume industry. As a young man, I had a particularly memorable sexual encounter with a girl who always wore a certain distinct scent. To this day, whenever I catch a whiff of that brand of perfume, it's all I can do to keep my pants from bursting at the seams. And it's not just man-made scents that the penis responds to, it's the perfumes of nature as well. Whatever blooms in spring surely plays a role in turning a young man's fancy. And many researchers believe that substances called pheromones, which are secreted when a woman is aroused, stimulate the male through the olfactory sense. We know this to be true in most animal species, and it just might be so with humans.

As for the other senses, consider the impact of certain *sounds*—romantic melodies, erotic rhythms, a gentle surf, a breeze rustling the trees outside the bedroom window—not to mention sweet, erotic words being whispered in your ear: "I have to have you"; "You're the sexiest man I've ever known"; "Do it to me." The penis responds as if it had ears of its own.

Think of the erotic appeal of certain *tastes:* moist tropical fruits, ice cubes, and of course your lover's sweat, saliva, and vaginal fluids.

As for *sight,* need I remind you what your penis does at the vision of the right woman in the right setting in the right clothing (or absence thereof)? Whether your taste is Frederick's of Hollywood or Victoria's Secret, whether it's tight jeans or a diaphanous skirt, a skimpy bikini or a beach towel wrapped around a mystery, that one-eyed creature between your legs responds to what you see.

Of course, arousal involves more than the senses; the mind and emotions are crucial players. The same stimuli that work like magic on one occasion might elicit indifference on another, depending on your mood and the psychological undercurrents. The strokes, scents, and sights of a woman you love, or one you've been lusting after, will produce vastly different effects than the strokes, scents, and sights of someone you can't stand. And, needless to say, arousal can occur without any help from the senses at all; *imagination* is often sufficient unto itself. Just ask anyone who had an adolescent penis; those hypersensitive devils are primed to spring forward at the slightest provocation, like car alarms that are triggered when someone stands too close.

STAND UP AND BE COUNTED

Whatever the source of arousal, what occurs is a complex physiological reaction involving nerves, muscles, blood vessels, and hormones. When the brain decides it is time for the penis to stand up and be counted, signals travel to the lumbar area of the spinal cord. From there, messages are dispatched along a network of nerves to the penis. The tiny muscles within the walls of the penile arteries are ordered to relax, opening up these channels and allowing more blood to flow in. Now bear in mind that blood is *always* flowing into the penis from the rest of the body, but it enters in relatively small amounts and it flows back out through the veins at a more or less steady pace. Hence, most of the time the penis stays soft. When you're aroused, however, blood gets pumped to where it's needed, gushing into the penis at six to eight times its normal rate. The penis becomes engorged: the arteries distend, the small sinusoids fill up, the corpora expand like balloons and press against the tunica in which they are encased. As a result, the penis not only gets bigger, but stiffer and more erect, just like a fire hose that goes from limp and bendable to hard and rigid as it fills with water. Just how big and how rigid the penis becomes depends on both how much *potential* volume the corpora were granted by heredity and how filled up they become, which depends on complex mental and physical factors.

In one of nature's most marvelous and elegant arrangements, the penis *stays* hard because the blood that has flooded in to cause *tumescence* does not flow back out. Unless the design is impeded by a physical abnormality or a psychological inhibition, the outflow of blood through the venous system is held in check by a valvelike mechanism so that the penis can stay hard long enough to do its business. It is as if the traffic lanes going into a parking lot were widened to allow more cars to enter, then, once the cars were in, those lanes were blocked off, preventing the traffic from flowing back out.

When ejaculation occurs, or when arousal is interrupted

for some reason (the phone rings, you get nervous, your partner complains that you're pulling her hair) the result is *detumescence.* The smooth muscles around the sinusoids and small arteries contract. The roadblocks in the venous system open up to allow blood to flow back out. The penis quickly and efficiently becomes flaccid again.

There is no greater symbol of masculinity than an erection; it is the anatomical equivalent of wealth, power, and strength. It is rescuing the damsel in distress, winning the ball game, defeating the bad guy in time to save the town, all wrapped into one five-to-seven-inch shaft of flesh and blood. Therefore, nothing carries with it more humiliation or self-recrimination than erectile malfunction. The reasons that an erection does not occur as desired are even more complex and varied than the reasons for it working properly, and I will discuss them in the next chapter.

COME AGAIN?

The goal for which nature designed erections is, of course, procreation. This is accomplished by the reflex of ejaculation, which is not to be confused with orgasm (although the two usually, but not always, go together like a horse and carriage). Orgasm refers to the intense feeling of pleasure and release that men and women experience at the climax of sexual excitement. It is principally neurological in nature, an electrochemical event centered in areas of the brain that govern pleasure. In our laboratories, we can trigger an orgasm in animals by stimulating their brains in the right way. Most of the time, men have orgasms when they ejaculate, or come, as it is known colloquially. However, at one time or another, most men have had the disconcerting experience of ejaculating without the pleasurable sensations of orgasm—perhaps when, as adolescents, they were so overwhelmed by excitement and anxiety that they came in their pants. And some men have experienced the reverse: orgasm without ejaculation. Reportedly, men who become adept at some esoteric Oriental sex practices can accomplish this, but many of my elderly patients have also experienced it—without trying and to their considerable chagrin—until they learn that it is perfectly normal.

By ejaculation, we mean the discharge of semen through the penis. This occurs through a reflex action involving a number of body parts. Let's begin with the manufacture of the substance itself, the semen, or the ejaculate.

WHERE IT'S COMING FROM

Contrary to popular belief, the sticky, milky-white fluid is not produced exclusively in the testicles. It is actually the contribution of three different organs, the *testicles*, the *seminal vesicles*, and the *prostate*. The component that the testicles provide is by far the smallest, albeit the most important: sperm. In a normal man, anywhere from 100 to 600 million sperm cells accompany each ejaculation in search of a fertilized ovary to impregnate. But those millions of cells constitute a minuscule percentage of the ejaculate volume.

Sperm travels from each testicle through a pair of tubes called the *vas deferens*, to be stored in the seminal vesicles. These vesicles are two pouches that stick out like pennant flags in a stiff wind behind the prostate and near the point where the urethra emerges from the bladder. There, the sperm is mixed with the rest of the seminal fluid, which is, essentially, a medium to transport the sperm. Some of the fluid is manufactured in the seminal vesicles themselves and the remaining portion is produced in the prostate gland, an oval-shaped organ about the size of a small plum, located at the neck of the bladder and surrounding the urethra. The prostate not only contributes to the content of the semen, but facilitates the process of ejaculation itself. It helps to shut off the flow of urine from the bladder when a man is aroused so that semen alone enters the penis.

Thus the complex products of the testicles, prostate, and seminal vesicles formulate the seminal fluid that is ejaculated at the climax of the sex act. However, we should mention another secretion that is actually the first to emerge. That honor belongs to a clear, sticky fluid manufactured in the *Cowper's glands*, which are about the size of peas and located just under the prostate. Small drops of the Cowper's fluid typically appear at the tip of the penis during the arousal stage. Some men confuse this with ejaculate, causing them to panic, thinking they are coming too quickly. Others know better, but make the mistake of assuming that the fluid contains no sperm cells. In fact, it might contain some—and only one is enough to impregnate an egg. The purpose of the fluid from the Cowper's glands is, we believe, to help lubricate the vagina. Nature doesn't miss a trick.

THE POINT OF NO RETURN

With sufficient stimulation to an erect penis, the reflex action of ejaculation is triggered. As you have no doubt discovered, the amount of time it takes for this to occur depends on the individual and the circumstances. The sensation of pleasure involved also varies; a man might experience fireworks or he might feel ho-hum. As far as we know, differences in the intensity and pleasure of orgasm are mediated in the brain and mainly entail psychological and emotional factors, such as novelty, love, romance, fantasy, physical chemistry, and the intensity of lovemaking that precedes the orgasm. But what takes place *physically* during ejaculation is always the same, with minor variations, whether a man is masturbating in a closet or making love under a tropical waterfall with the woman of his dreams.

What happens is this: when a certain level of excitement is reached, a complex chain of nerve impulses signals the muscles in the pelvic floor to contract. These muscles are located in the perineum, the area between the back of the scrotum and the bottom of the rectum (it's often referred to as the "'tain't," as in, "'Tain't your balls and 'tain't your anus"). These contractions close the neck of the bladder and open the ejaculatory ducts so that sperm and seminal fluid can enter the urethra, where the components are combined. The pelvic contractions are accompanied by muscle contractions in other parts of the body (such as the lower back and abdomen) and by an increase in the heart and respiratory rates, making ejaculation a whole-body phenomenon.

It is at this point, when the contractions of the perineal muscles forcefully start to move the semen on its route through the penis, that men feel the sensations that tell them they are about to come. From this point on, ejaculation is inevitable. It is a pure reflex that can't be stopped. Therefore, as we shall see, any effort to delay ejaculation has to be made *prior* to this point of no return.

The ejaculate is powerfully propelled from the back of the urethra through the penis and out the tip. It squirts out in several jellylike clumps, which quickly liquefy into an opaque fluid to help the sperm swim to the ovary. Exactly how much is ejaculated varies with factors like age (less semen the older you get) and the length of time since the previous ejaculation (more semen the longer it's been). Statistically, the amount of seminal fluid per ejaculate ranges from one and a half to five cubic centimeters and averages about three cc's, which is about a teaspoon. The volume ejaculated decreases with age, because the body simply produces less. The forcefulness of the ejaculation also decreases with age, due to a natural decline in muscular strength and changes in the vascular system. Hence, whereas a young man might project five cc's of ejaculate halfway across a room, an older man might just dribble a few drops, but the mechanism is exactly the same.

It is important to realize that there is absolutely no correlation between the volume of ejaculate and the amount of pleasure that is experienced. Some men actually allow themselves to feel disappointed if they don't produce barrels of the stuff because, for reasons of ignorance, they learned to link their masculinity to the volume of semen they produce. Some actually complain to me that their sex lives are lousy because they don't ejaculate as much as they used to. When I tell them that *everyone* produces less as they age and that it has nothing whatsoever to do with pleasure, one of two things happen: they either start enjoying sex again because they are relieved of this self-imposed psychological burden, or they are forced to focus on the *real* problem, which can be anything from a conflict with their spouses to a correctable medical condition.

There does seem to be a relationship between the strength and duration of the perineal contractions and the intensity of pleasure, and for that reason I will describe, in a later chapter, certain exercises to strengthen the perineal muscles. But I must emphasize this important point: any difference in the satisfaction of one ejaculation as compared to another is centered overwhelmingly between your ears, not between your legs or in your perineum. A particular orgasm might *feel* especially satisfying because of the intensity of emotions involved, or the partner's sexual skills, or the circumstances surrounding the experience. It is not because of the volume of seminal fluid. If an orgasm that is accompanied by a large amount of semen *does* feel unusually intense it is for a good reason: chances are the man has gone a long time between ejaculations. The longer you go, the more fluid is built up in the seminal vesicles and the more sexual "tension" you feel based on overdistension of the storage pouches. When you finally ejaculate, you relieve that built-up volume, and that is why it feels so good.

"I WANT TO BE ALONE"

As soon as ejaculation is completed, the process is reversed. The heart beat, blood pressure, and respiratory rate gradually slow down to resting levels. You feel sated and relaxed, perhaps sleepy. The scrotum, which reflexively contracts during sexual arousal, and the testes, which rise up within the scrotal sac, relax into their customary position. As for the penis, as the blood drains out it reverts to its flaccid state, as if it wants to retreat into solitude and not be seen. Also, the head of the penis becomes extremely sensitive. It doesn't want to be touched. It doesn't want to be sucked. It might even burn or hurt if it makes contact with anything. It's as if, after ejaculation, the penis dons a neon sign reading, LEAVE ME ALONE!

This is a time of rest, when the male body restores itself before it can once again be aroused. During what is called the *refractory period,* no amount of stimulation will produce an erection or ejaculation. Exactly how long it takes for your equipment to be restored varies considerably from one man to another. And any given man will notice distinct variations in his refractory period, depending on his partner, the circumstances, and factors such as fatigue and general health. The two main variables that determine the length of the refractory period are age and the length of time since the previous ejaculation. Generally speaking, men need more time to rest the older they get. The same man who, at nineteen, was ready to go five minutes after ejaculating might need an hour at age forty and a full day at age sixty. And a man who has gone without sex for a long period of time will be restored much more quickly than if he has just ejaculated for the tenth time in two days.

The refractory period is nature's way of making sure men don't waste their energy when they have no semen to contribute, for it is during the rest phase that the seminal vesicles fill up again. These vesicles act like a reservoir with a feedback system. When they are empty, or the volume of seminal fluid is low, the body starts producing more. During that phase a man will feel little if any desire and will not respond to efforts to arouse him. As the supply of semen is replenished, the seminal vesicles become distended, and when they are filled up seminal production is curtailed. The refractory period is, for all intents and purposes, over.

The distended vesicles then trigger a neurological signal that produces a sense of "pressure" in the perineum. That is what produces the common feeling of being "horny." Now that neon sign on the penis is shut off, the little guy perks up, raises his head, and starts calling attention to itself.

* * *

That, then, is the basic anatomy of erection and ejaculation, assuming that everything goes right. It is, of course,
those moments when it *doesn't* go right—when the physiology
of erection doesn't kick in as expected, or the mechanism of
detumescence occurs at inopportune moments, or ejaculation is
untimely—that all men dread, so let's turn our attention to
that important area.

6

When the Spirit Is Willing but the Body Is Not

Years ago, in the heyday of Freud, it was assumed that impotence was a psychological problem. A man who could not get an erection had to be psychoanalyzed to find out the deep, dark roots of his neurosis. Then we learned that erection problems could be caused by medical disorders. Since then, we have developed sophisticated tools for distinguishing between organic impotence and penis weakness caused by psychological or situational factors. And in cases where the cause is clearly physical, we can also diagnose the precise cause.

The sexual problems men report to me fall into three basic categories: desire, erection, and ejaculation. Concerns about diminished desire usually come from middle-aged or elderly men who are distressed that they do not crave sex as much as they once did. Concerns about ejaculation come in two types: too fast and too slow; in medical jargon, premature and retarded. Quick-on-the-trigger complaints are heard mainly from younger men, while the too-slow variety come from their elders. With rare exceptions, problems with desire and ejaculation are not treatable medical disorders, but are handled psychologically or behaviorally. In fact, in many cases a patient with such complaints doesn't actually have a problem, but is simply misinformed about what is normal and what can reasonably be expected.

In this chapter I will focus on medical conditions that affect penis power. But first, a few general points must be made.

DON'T BE SICKER THAN YOU REALLY ARE

In a sense, any illness can have a dampening impact on a man's potency. The general weakness and fatigue that accompanies sickness will naturally affect your sex drive and your ability to respond to stimulation. Also, depending on the nature of the affliction and its severity, a patient's range of movement might be too limited to engage in normal sex. And in many cases illness brings with it a certain amount of depression or despair, a feeling of inadequacy, and an image of one's body as impaired, all of which can diminish penis power even if the illness itself does not.

Unfortunately, many sick men give up on themselves as sexual beings, convincing themselves that they are no longer capable of virile, manly activities. They might also become overprotective, refraining from all exertion—even from sex-related exercises that might do their condition a world of good. Arthritis victims, for example, sometimes abstain from sex because the pain in their joints prevents them from moving around as vigorously as they would like. They are not only depriving themselves of some much-needed and well-deserved joy, but possibly an improved range of motion and relief from pain as well. My rheumatology colleagues tell me that there is evidence that arthritis sufferers can experience relief from pain for four to six hours after an orgasm.

Unfortunately, some physicians play into this negative mind-set. They advise their patients to limit their sexual activity or even give it up entirely when illness strikes. A doctor who goes by the book might even tell a patient that he'll never have "normal sexual relations" again. What a terrible way to put it! Patients not only get depressed when they hear this, but take it literally and think they have to retire their penises and give up all sexual and sensual pleasures entirely. Furthermore, the doctor's negative prognosis is often erroneous. Not long ago physicians told heart patients and people with back pain to avoid exercise; now we prescribe exercise programs for their rehabilitation and advise against being sedentary. In many cases the same is true of sex. I advise and encourage my patients to use their penises to bring cheer to the sickbed, rather than allow the penis to shrivel up before its time.

If your doctor tells you to abstain from exercising your penis power, get a second opinion! He might be misinformed or simply old-fashioned. His advice might deprive you of something that is more soothing and healing than a good laugh. In my experience, illness might limit your sexuality, but it does not have to eliminate it. In many cases, it is merely a question of learning new habits. Your condition might mean it takes longer to achieve an erection, for example, in which case you can learn to be more patient and your partner can learn new ways to stimulate you. Your illness might make it impossible to make love in the positions you are accustomed to. If so, practice new ones. You might have to have sex less often or less vigorously, but instead of lamenting that situation, you can learn to fully savor the slow, gentle sensuality you used to hurry through. If you have intercourse less often, you might be able to enjoy oral sex or mutual masturbation *more* often. Such changes make sex different, not inferior. They should be viewed as opportunities for new experiences, rather than reasons to feel sorry for yourself or give up one of life's great pleasures.

"MY FRIEND HAS THIS PROBLEM..."

Very few things are tougher for a man to do than admit he's having erection problems. Even confiding it to a physician is so embarrassing that men put it off as long as they can, sometimes until it is too late to correct the situation easily. Women can't possibly understand the humiliation a man feels when, in the midst of passionate foreplay, his penis does not get erect—or an erect penis suddenly and without warning goes limp. When a woman doesn't lubricate, she can reach for the K-Y Jelly or her partner can use saliva. Even if she is not terribly aroused a woman can proceed with intercourse, and if she wants to she can always *pretend* to be passionate. A man without an erection has no such fallback position. With his penis drooping like a flag on a windless day, he's stripped bare of all pretense. No artifice can compensate. This, for most men, is a nightmare worse than dropping a touchdown pass in the end zone or striking out with the bases loaded. Even if it happens once it can be devastating, since very few men are able to shrug it off. And when it happens more than once, the shake-up to self-esteem is high on a man's Richter scale. They *should* shrug it off, however, because it happens from time to time to everyone.

So when a man comes to my office and tells me he is having trouble getting or keeping an erection I know how hard it is for him to make that admission. The first thing I do is try to make him comfortable. I quickly try to earn his trust with an understanding smile and a warm demeanor, so he can speak openly and honestly about this most delicate situation. Having established rapport, I take a medical history. The first thing I want to know is whether his problem with erections is of recent origin or has been going on for a long time. I also want to know if the onset was sudden or gradual. Depending on his answers, I then ask a series of questions about his personal life and state of mind. I follow an algorithm, in which the patient's answers guide each subsequent question, leading to an accurate diagnosis. You would be surprised how many men come to me in a complete penis panic only to find out their problem isn't medical at all, but something circumstantial, like a marriage on the rocks, aggravation over a business predicament, or plain fatigue.

At this point, if my analysis has not revealed an obvious situational cause, my line of inquiry turns to medical factors. When the penis fails to perform up to expected standards and psychological factors are ruled out, the diagnosis falls into the clinical category of organic impotence. Even though only a small portion of the men who come to me with sexual complaints fall into this category, my first responsibility as a urologist is to search for a possible medical cause for the problem penis.

Before embarking on a sophisticated medical evaluation, I have to be convinced that the patient is, in fact, physically incapable of having an erection. This is often accomplished with one question. For example, take the case of a fifty-year-old executive who came to me with a minor irritation on his scrotal skin. I prescribed a topical ointment and then listened as this aggressive, no-nonsense mover and shaker gazed at the floor and sheepishly told me the real reason for his visit to my office: "Doc, I just can't get it up lately." He said he felt fine otherwise and was not under any exceptional degree of stress.

At that moment, my secretary buzzed to tell me that the lab assistant had stopped by to pick up a blood sample. Knowing that this assistant was a beautiful young woman (a knockout, in fact) I seized the opportunity to use a visual aid to solve the diagnostic enigma. When the assistant entered the exam area, we exchanged pleasantries, I handed her the sample, and she left. I watched as my patient eyed her shapely figure as it swayed out the door. "If she came on to you," I asked, "do you think you would have any problem rising to the occasion?"

"Are you kidding, Doc?" said the patient. "When do we start?"

The medical problem was solved. His penis weakness was within his marital bedroom and not some anatomic malfunction in his organ. Of course a remark like that does not constitute scientific proof, but in this patient's case there was other evidence. He confessed to having had a recent fling with a woman he met on a business trip. During the affair he performed adequately. Virtually certain that the patient was not physically impaired, I counseled him along psychological lines and suggested that he and his wife might want to see a marital therapist.

For most patients the question of whether a penis problem is physical or mental cannot be settled in an interview. As a physician I have to use reliable, objective criteria. And in fact I have a foolproof method at my disposal.

To Sleep, Perchance to Get Hard

Fact: all *healthy* males get erections during their sleep, every night without exception. Each episode lasts about half an hour, although the penis is not fully erect the entire time. All healthy men, regardless of age, get these nocturnal erections four or five times a night, in cycles, separated by one to two hours. Most of them coincide with the REM (for "rapid eye movement") stage of sleep. This is the period during which dreaming occurs, but the erections are not associated with the content of dreams. They are totally nonsexual in nature; even infants have them.

I don't want to create the false impression that a twenty-year-old sleeping penis acts the same as its sixty-year-old counterpart. The total *time* of nocturnal tumescence and the *duration* of each erection are age-related; they are longest during the teenage years, after which they gradually decline. However, I can assure you that normal, healthy men in their eighties still have three or four erections per night. All of which means that on the average the penis of a medically fit man is erect more than 100 minutes a night.

Urologists don't quite know what the purpose of these nocturnal erections is or what function, if any, they serve in the sleep process. But thankfully they give us an important diagnostic tool. We assume that these nonsexual sleep erections occur by the same mechanisms that cause sexual erections. Therefore we reason that if a man has normal erections during sleep he is anatomically and physiologically capable of having good erections during sex. In which case, we can safely conclude that his penis weakness is not rooted in any organic condition but is instead psychological in origin. In reverse, if the patient does *not* have normal sleep erections, we conclude that some organic condition is impeding the process, and our diagnosis is organic impotence.

If one of my patients happens to wake up in the middle of the night and finds his penis at attention, or if he has an erection when he wakes up in the morning (the condition sometimes referred to as a "piss hard-on" because the morning erection is often accompanied by the need to urinate), he will have the luxury of knowing that his penis is in good working order. But urologists have a more convincing way to make this determination—a diagnostic procedure called the nocturnal penile tumescence test (NPT).

We give the patient a simple kit to take home with him. It consists of a state-of-the-art gadget with loops that look like a small pair of blood pressure cuffs. These are attached around the penis, one at the base and one just under the glans. Comfortable enough to sleep with but secure enough not to fall off, the gauges are attached by wire to a meter, which in turn is hooked up to a printer, like the ones you have seen used in lie detector tests. If the patient's penis enlarges, as it would with a normal nocturnal erection, the pressure inside the cuffs increases and the change registers in graph form on the recording device. With this tool we can actually measure the increase in diameter and the degree of rigidity of the penis.

This simple device tells me whether a patient is *physically* capable of achieving a satisfactory erection. Regardless of the outcome, my patients invariably feel better because now, at last, the mystery and torment have been resolved. They either feel relieved to discover that they can, in fact, have an erection and that there is nothing wrong medically, or they are relieved to find out that the problem is physical, not mental. Once I know that the problem is physical, I can proceed to diagnose the actual nature of the disorder and outline an appropriate treatment plan.

It is interesting to note that before we had sophisticated monitoring devices I relied on a simple, homemade procedure that can still be used by patients who are intimidated by machines. Take a roll of postage stamps and wrap it around your penis before you go to sleep. If when you awaken in the morning the perforation between the stamps is torn, there is a good chance you had an erection during the night. The postage stamp test, though scientifically crude, is fairly reliable.

If the patient fails to get an adequate nighttime erection, then it is time for me to proceed with a complete urologic evaluation. Thanks to some remarkable medical advances, physical disorders that used to go undetected can now be diagnosed and the men who suffer from them can be treated medically. In the old days such men might have spent years in psychotherapy to no avail while their self-esteem and penis power plummeted to even greater depths. The key is to obtain an accurate diagnosis, and in most cases we can determine the cause in our offices. There are basically three categories of disorders that cause penis failure: neurological, vascular, and hormonal. I must again emphasize that, for all the penis weakness I see in my practice, organic causes are responsible for only a small number.

NEUROLOGICAL DISORDERS

Some patients are incapable of generating or sustaining an erection because of impairments in the complex network of nerves that make an erection possible. In almost all such cases, the impotence is a symptom of a preexisting neurological disorder, among them multiple sclerosis, Parkinson's, cervical disc disease, and tumors or injuries of the spinal cord. In addition, conditions such as long-term alcoholism and advanced diabetes can lead to damage of the peripheral nerves and impair erections.

When a patient's medical history reveals any of these disorders and nocturnal erections do not occur, then neurological failure is suspected. To verify this I might perform a simple exam called the bulbocavernosus reflex test. I insert a gloved finger into the patient's anal sphincter, then with my other hand gently squeeze the tip of the penis. If the reflex arc is working properly, the anal sphincter will contract firmly against my examining finger. With this simple test I determine if the reflex arc necessary for erection is functional.

Some neurological conditions that cause penis weakness

are correctable. For example, if a damaged cervical disc is surgically corrected or a spinal tumor is removed, the patient might recover normal function. Sadly, however, most neurological causes of penis failure are not correctable and are outside the province of the urologist's expertise. We usually refer such patients to neurologists or neurosurgeons for further assessment and treatment, if possible.

Vascular Disorders

Of all the *medical* causes of penis dysfunction, by far the most common are vascular diseases. As we saw earlier, an erection is in large part a function of blood flow. Problems can be caused by obstructions in the arteries that bring blood to the penis, or by leaks in the venous system that result when the blood in the shaft drains out prematurely. In other words, if not enough blood enters your penis or not enough is held there, your penis can't stay erect. Consequently, one of the first things I look for in my patient's medical history is evidence of cardiovascular disease—high blood pressure, chest pain (angina), pain in the legs after walking or exercise (called claudication) —all related to conditions that gum up the blood vessels of your body, and most assuredly those that serve the penis. For that reason, by the way, one of the most important things a man who aspires to penis power can do is maintain good cardiovascular fitness through diet, weight control, and exercise.

By discussing the patient's symptoms with him, I can get a good idea of whether to look further for possible vascular disturbances. In years past it was extremely difficult to identify vascular defects in the erection process. The tests were time-consuming and difficult to perform and interpret. All that has changed. We now have several simple, accurate techniques for identifying vascular problems.

One simple technique entails measuring penile blood pressure. We use essentially the same technology as the familiar blood pressure cuff, only this band is a lot smaller than the one that fits around your bicep. We measure the blood pressure in the penis and that in the brachial artery in the arm (the site of routine blood pressure testing) and get a ratio called the penile-brachial index (PBI). Normally, penile blood pressure is equal to or greater than the brachial. If it is significantly lower, we consider it a reliable indication of failed blood flow to the penis. In some cases, we also measure the PBI before and after the patient exercises on a stationary bicycle in the office. A decrease in the PBI is evidence of a "pelvic steal." It suggests that blood destined for the penis is being diverted to the legs.

A newer, more sophisticated method for identifying arterial insufficiency is the Doppler pulse-wave analysis. This instrument produces an ultrasound beam that we direct toward the blood vessels in the penis. The motion of the blood cells bounces a signal back to the instrument, and the signal varies depending on the volume of blood flowing through the vessel. The signal is either amplified into an audible sound or recorded as waves on a chart. The procedure is noninvasive, painless, and extremely precise. Thus, without having to attach gadgets to the penis itself, we can even measure the blood flow through individual arteries.

Still more advanced, albeit more invasive, is a method called penile arteriography. We inject a dye into the artery that supplies the penis and monitor the blood flow with X-ray equipment that is sensitive to the dye. This is by far the most accurate way to assess the minute arteries that supply blood to the penis during erection. However, we do not do it routinely since it requires anesthetizing the patient and injecting the dye directly into a very small artery, sometimes producing unwanted complications. In my practice, I reserve this procedure for a few selected cases, such as patients with major pelvic injuries or isolated arterial damage that might be amenable to surgical repair.

In the early 1980s, a revolutionary technique was introduced with major positive implications for both diagnosis and treatment. It entails injecting into the penis specific vasoactive drugs, i.e., drugs that dilate the penile arteries. This dramatically increases blood flow to the penis, usually producing an immediate erection regardless of mental factors and even in the face of significant systemic blood vessel disease. The most commonly used injectable drugs are papaverine and prostaglandin E. In my experience, the injections are the best way to screen for circulatory problems. With one simple injection, we can determine whether the arterial system is intact. The penis either gets hard or it does not.

Sometimes we use these injections in combination with a procedure called the radioisotope penogram. We inject a harmless radioactive material into the penis. Then, using a camera that is sensitive to radioactive material, we can obtain an accurate, quantifiable measurement of blood flow through the penis. Normal patients will exhibit a marked increase in radioactivity, whereas those with impaired blood flow will not. Nowadays, this method is seldom used to diagnose vascular problems, but rather to evaluate the results of treatment procedures.

If my patient gets only partial erections, or loses them when he changes position, I might also suspect problems with blood flow *out* of the penis—a venous leak. In some cases, blood flows into the penis normally, but is not held in the corpora within the shaft long enough to sustain erection because the valve mechanism in the veins is not working adequately to trap the blood. New X-ray technology enables us to diagnose a venous leak.

For me, these harmless, painless methods for measuring penodynamics represent a medical miracle. Now that we can measure the blood flow through each and every vessel in the penis, we can accurately diagnose blood vessel obstructions and leaks. Even more amazing, we can take precise steps to correct these problems. Later I will describe the use of papaverine and prostaglandin injections to restore declining penis power, especially in aging men (see Chapter Seven).

HORMONAL DISORDERS

By far the most common endocrine disease associated with penis failure is diabetes. Diabetes is a syndrome characterized by the abnormal secretion of insulin, which precisely regulates the amount of circulating blood sugar. It is a major cause of generalized arteriosclerosis (hardening of the arteries) and widespread neuropathy, a disorder that destroys nerves throughout the body. With respect to penis power, diabetes is a double threat: it can cause severe damage to the blood vessels and to nerves going to the penis. A significant number of my young diabetic male patients experience a gradual decrease in the *sensitivity* of their penises and a decline in the firmness of their erections. Tragically, many diabetics ultimately become entirely incapable of normal sexual functioning.

I must emphasize that not every diabetic is doomed to penis weakness. If diabetes is diagnosed early and is properly managed with diet, oral medication, insulin injections, and exercise, there is a good chance of restoring penis power—or never having it weaken at all.

Other hormonal conditions can also affect penis power. These include abnormal thyroid function—either an underactive or an overactive thyroid gland; overproduction of the hormone prolactin, which is usually a side effect of certain medications; tumors in the pituitary gland; or a deficiency of testosterone, the male sex hormone. Once diagnosed, these conditions are all easily correctable.

In a small number of my patients a blood-screening test might reveal abnormally low levels of male hormone (testosterone). Most patients who develop this condition have suffered a testicular injury or had the mumps virus as a child. Mumps can lead to orchitis, an inflammation that causes the testicles to atrophy, rendering them deficient in testosterone production. These patients are treated with periodic injections of testosterone to bring it up to normal levels. This works effectively to restore the patient's full penis power. The key here is to recognize testicular failure as the cause.

I must emphasize that there is no legitimate reason to use testosterone if the circulating blood level is already within the normal range. Contrary to the belief of many of my patients, the hormone will *not* improve the penis performance of someone whose level is normal to begin with. Not only that, testosterone and its derivatives, the notorious anabolic steroids, can cause serious side effects. If a man whose testosterone level is within the normal range consumes additional amounts either orally or by injection, a signal is sent to the testicles to produce *less* of the male hormone. Through a complex feedback mechanism, the body is fine-tuned to maintain just the right amount of circulating testosterone. It can use only so much of it. If you add some from the outside, the body's computer says, "Hey, I'm getting all this testosterone. I'd better tell the testicles to stop producing the stuff." The result: "tiny testes."

The widespread use of steroids by athletes and bodybuilders is alarming enough; to think that some men might take them in the vain hope of improving their penis power is even more distressing. In my practice I have seen several terrific male specimens—athletes and movie stars whose bodies look like sculpted marble—who discovered to their horror that steroids were destroying their fertility and their sex lives. Their testicles had shrunk to the size of peas. It is not worth it, even for men whose fortune depends on their muscular images. For the average man to take anabolic steroids, like testosterone or its derivatives, in the hope that it will turn him into a stud is utter madness.

DRUGS AND PENIS POWER

PRESCRIPTION DRUGS

A television producer whom I had treated for a urinary infection came to see me. The minute I walked into the examining room I knew from his facial expression that he had not come about the infection. Whatever was on his mind was serious, and not something he found easy to talk about. When he finally said, "Doctor, I can't get hard anymore," I was shocked. He had a reputation as a cocksman of note and he took great pride in his penis power.

We talked for a while about what was going on in his life. I explored the possibility that he, as a single man who liked a variety of partners, might feel frightened by the AIDS epidemic. He rejected that; he was careful to sleep with carefully screened partners and practice only safe sex. I thought he might be under some stress or physical strain, given the demands of his profession. But he assured me that his life was no more pressured than before, when he had no penis problems and, in fact, used sex as an outlet for his built-up tension. His recent failures were unprecedented and he couldn't figure out what had happened.

When I took his medical history in preparation for a complete examination, I hit upon the answer. Since I had last seen him he had been diagnosed with high blood pressure. But it wasn't the hypertension that was affecting his penis power, it was the prescription medication he was taking to control it.

A number of therapeutic drugs can cause erection or ejaculation problems, even in men with excellent penis attitudes. Unfortunately, very few rigorous scientific studies have been performed, so most of what we know about penis weakness associated with the use of common medicines is anecdotal or reported by manufacturers as possible side effects. When I suspect that a drug might be responsible for a patient's problem I do an informal test, reducing the dosage or eliminating the drug entirely to see if the patient's penis power is restored. Naturally, this is done with the cooperation of the primary physician, with all possible safeguards observed. In the case of the TV producer, not long after we lowered the dosage of his antihypertensive medicine he was back to his old tricks.

Blood pressure medications are not the only culprit, although they are probably the most common. If you were to peruse the *Physician's Desk Reference* (the bible of drug side effects), you would see that sexual dysfunction is listed as a potential side effect of virtually every antihypertensive agent. The medications work in different ways to lower blood pressure, hence their effects on the penis also vary. For example, the incidence of penis weakness among those taking reserpine is as high as 30 to 40 percent; those taking guanethidine have a 40 percent chance of having ejaculatory malfunction and about a 20 percent chance of having erection failure. If you are taking antihypertensive agents and suspect they are adversely affecting your penis power, consult with your physician. You might be able to switch to a class of drug whose ingredients will not keep you from being a superpotent man.

Other drugs that can diminish penis power include some diuretics. Certain medications used to treat anxiety, depression, and other psychiatric disturbances can cause diminished libido, retarded ejaculation, or erection problems. Various ulcer medications can also cause impotency in some patients because they disrupt the production of testosterone.

I must caution anyone taking prescription medication not to give it up arbitrarily or alter the dosage. If you suspect that your penis power has been affected by a drug, consult with your physician before doing anything on your own. This is an extremely complicated area. Even a well-trained physician is not always able to tell with certainty whether the medication is causing the problem. Many forces might be contributing to your inability to get an erection, not just the medication. Many patients who take such drugs are of advanced age, suffer from more than one illness, take a variety of medications, and have other habits that could affect their penis power.

Then there is the underlying disease itself. High blood pressure can weaken penis power in and of itself; indeed, approximately 10 percent of patients who require antihypertensive drugs have significant penis weakness *before* starting treatment. Similarly, depression can cause sexual dysfunction. How can we be certain whether it is the disease, the drug, or a combination of both? Moreover, the sexual side effects of the drugs have to be weighed against the consequences of the diseases themselves. In some cases, switching medications or adjusting the dosage is an easy solution. However, when that is not possible it might be wiser to live with diminished penis power than to risk aggravating a serious medical condition by disrupting treatment. Such decisions require delicate clinical judgment, which is why it is important to have a frank, thorough discussion with your physician and a rigorous scrutiny of all possible options.

RECREATIONAL DRUGS

Scenarios like the one with the TV producer have been repeated many times in my office, not only with prescription drugs but with so-called recreational substances. Addiction or abuse can cause everything from temporary penis failure to long-term impotence, and the culprits are many. Some drugs provide the *illusion* of enhanced sexuality because they take the edge off, calm you down, and lower inhibitions. But to repeat Shakespeare's observation, drugs might add to desire but they take away from performance.

As the old expression goes, "Candy is dandy, but liquor is quicker." We all know the routine. You have a few drinks and everything from your tongue to your toes loosens up. Wallflowers start to dance, the tongue-tied become candid and verbose, the sexually uptight become Lotharios. And if the object of your attention has also been drinking, suddenly everything becomes possible. For those reasons, alcohol has become as much a part of lovemaking for some people as soft lights. There is nothing dangerous about moderate, judicious drinking; if it reduces anxiety, slows you down, and delays ejaculation a bit, alcohol can be a boon to penis power. Unfortunately, it can also be your penis's greatest enemy. If you overdo it, your penis will poop when it ought to pop.

Then there are the effects of alcohol on abusers: it is more difficult to become aroused, it takes longer to ejaculate, the pleasure and intensity of orgasms are reduced, and penis rigidity is greatly diminished. Up to 50 percent of chronic alcoholics experience either total or partial impotence. The short-term effects appear to be based on alcohol's sedative action on the central nervous system. The long-term or chronic effects, which have been well documented, include severe nerve damage of the sort that can diminish penis sensitivity and impair the ability to get an erection.

A number of patients have told me that marijuana enhances their penis power. My hunch is that the effects are similar to those of alcohol. Studies have indicated that marijuana slows the ejaculatory process, hence an erection can be maintained for a longer period of time before orgasm. For a younger man who might be quick on the trigger this can be perceived as enhanced potency. In addition, marijuana might lower inhibitory mechanisms, reduce anxiety, and heighten erotic sensations.

However, I must recommend extreme caution about jumping to the conclusion that marijuana is an aphrodisiac or an aid to penis power. For one thing, since it is a mind-altering substance, its effect on sexuality might be illusory. Second, I suspect that, like alcohol, it would be antithetical to penis power in the long run. There is some evidence that long-term marijuana smoking weakens overall fitness and reduces energy and motivation. Such effects would not bode well for a superpotent man.

When Cole Porter wrote "I get no kick from cocaine" he might not have been thinking about sex, but the message applies: where penis power is concerned, cocaine is certainly no kick. In the short term it has an excitatory effect on the nervous system. It can stimulate arousal and make every sensory experience *seem* more intense. But in the long run cocaine is anathema to penis power. It will turn a superpotent man into a superwimp. Pharmacologically, cocaine decreases the reuptake of the neurotransmitter catecholamine, which is essential for the adequate completion of the erection process. Failure to get and maintain erections is a common complaint from abusers. No man who aspires to penis power should go anywhere near the drug.

As for other illicit drugs, no superpotent man should require them. With respect to amphetamines, remember the 1960s poster: Speed kills. It certainly kills libido, ejaculatory function, and erections. Its long-term sexual impact is devastating, as is the case for drugs in the narcotic family such as heroin, codeine, and Demerol. Universally, users of these drugs experience a drastic reduction in libido as well as chronic difficulty with erections. Unquestionably, these recreational drugs produce the antithesis of penis power.

One more drug must be mentioned, especially since it has long been associated with mating rituals: nicotine. As if there weren't enough reasons to stop smoking, or never start, consider this: smoking has been linked to penis weakness. Several studies have demonstrated that cigarette smoking is more prevalent among impotent men. In another study, animals exposed to tobacco smoke or intravenous nicotine were unable to produce or maintain erections. There is a scientific reason for this and it is simple: nicotine constricts blood vessels. When you smoke, the supply of arterial blood to the penis is reduced, making it more difficult to get a firm erection. Bottom line: smoking is as bad for your penis as it is for your lungs. If you want to be a penis power guy, just say no to nicotine.

PROSTATE AND OTHER UROLOGIC DISEASES

Jerry was a sixty-six-year-old chemistry professor who came to see me because he was having difficulty voiding. He was waking up three or four times a night to urinate, his urine flow was slow and irregular, and he felt a sensation of incomplete bladder emptying. These are signs suggestive of an enlarged prostate, a common condition in older men. The prostate is like a collar or donut that surrounds the neck of the bladder. You can envision the bladder as an upside-down balloon. As a man gets older, the prostate tends to get bigger, which means the hole in the donut gets smaller. The shrinking hole pinches the neck of the bladder, making it more difficult to urinate and causing the bladder to work harder to empty itself. This can lead to other symptoms besides the ones Jerry reported, such as blood in the urine, a dribbling urinary stream, painful urination, occasional incontinence, and sometimes pain in the lower back, pelvis, or lower abdomen.

I took a detailed medical history from Jerry, after which I performed a rectal examination with my educated gloved finger to assess the size and consistency of his prostate. I then used a device that measures the urinary flow rate and the patient's ability to completely empty his bladder. An ultrasound test, which projects sound waves through the prostate to search for signs of cancer, turned out negative.

Finally, I used a cystoscope, an amazing instrument that is inserted directly into the urinary channel and serves as a telescope. With the help of different lenses, I can actually examine the entire length of the urethra, and look directly at the prostate and into the bladder. This enables me to check for tumors, polyps, stones, and other causes of irritation, plus it allows me to assess the size and degree of prostatic obstruction.

Like most patients, Jerry was alarmed when I told him I wanted to use the cystoscope. "You're going to stick what in where?" he gasped. I assured him there would be no harm and no pain. With a simple local anesthesia, the procedure is entirely painless. It can be done in the office skillfully in less than a minute. In fact, I told him that if we hurt him at all there would be no charge—a promise I make without hesitation, and I do not like to work for free.

Following this complete examination, I concluded that Jerry's prostate was enlarged to the point where damage might eventually be done to his bladder or his kidneys. I recommended surgery, a prostatectomy. Jerry panicked. He started sweating heavily and stammering. Not because he was afraid of being under the knife, not because he didn't trust me to perform the surgery (which I had done successfully on thousands of patients, including Jerry's older brother and uncle), but because he thought that the operation would render him a penis weakling.

Jerry's reaction is so common among men with prostate disease—indeed, with any kind of problem in the pelvic area—that I must state in capital letters: PROSTATECTOMY, WHEN

DONE FOR BENIGN DISEASE, DOES NOT CAUSE IMPOTENCE OR ANY LOSS OF PENIS POWER!

Nowadays, prostate operations for benign disease do not even require a surgical incision. My preferred method is the transurethral prostatectomy (TURP). Virtually all benign prostatic obstruction can be cured in this manner, which some of my patients have dubbed "the roto-rooter technique." As with the cystoscope, the TURP involves entering the body through the urinary channel. A cutting and coagulating device is inserted that enables me, in essence, to core out the compressed hole in the donut. With a looped wire, I shave that portion of prostatic tissue that is obstructing the flow of urine. The method is quick, relatively painless, and by far the simplest and safest method of relieving prostate obstruction. The patient is usually out of the hospital in one, two, or occasionally three days, and the recovery period is brief. Unlike the old procedure, which required an abdominal incision, the likelihood of postoperative penis weakness is virtually nil.

If, like Jerry, you are a superpotent man capable of getting firm erections *before* a TURP, you will still be so afterward. In fact, it is possible that your penis power will be enhanced. Not because of anything the surgery does to your genitals, but because some of the consequences of prostate enlargement—i.e., distended bladder, abdominal bloating, pelvic pain, rectal pressure—can reduce your general well-being and with it your sexuality. In my experience, because the quality of life of a patient can improve after transurethral prostate surgery, his penis power might also be expected to improve.

In sum, do not hesitate to correct a prostate problem with routine surgery because you fear the loss of penis power. Your fear is unjustified. The prostate is a secondary sex organ. It is not directly responsible for erection or ejaculation. If you are scheduled for prostatic surgery, you can look forward to sitting through a movie and sleeping through the night without having to run to the bathroom, knowing that your penis will continue to bring you the pleasures you had before.

There is, however, one possible side effect of a TURP that

must be mentioned: retrograde ejaculation. In about 30 percent of post-TURP patients, little or no semen comes out of the penis. Instead, when the patient climaxes, semen is ejaculated *backward* into the bladder. This is harmless; the ejaculate is evacuated with the next voiding. Naturally, retrograde ejaculation presents an obstacle to fertility. However, with respect to penis power, the condition is more disturbing psychologically than medically. It does not affect the sensation of orgasm. A few of my patients have told me that backward ejaculation "makes sex about 10 percent less fun." I can't personally vouch for that estimate, but I suspect that the minor reduction in enjoyment is because the men feel strange, not because of any physical difference. Usually, they get used to it and even laugh about the fact that their partners find sex far less messy than it was in the old days. In any event, retrograde ejaculation is a small annoyance to accept for the sake of curing benign prostate enlargement and obstruction.

THE DREADED C WORD

Other diseases that afflict the genitourinary system carry with them a greater threat, both to life and penis power. I refer principally to cancer.

Recently, the rate of prostate cancer among men caught up to lung cancer. About one in every eleven men in the United States will develop the disease during his lifetime. The rate of incidence increases dramatically with age; 80 percent of those afflicted are over sixty-five. Treatment depends on a number of factors, including the patient's physical condition and the type and stage of the cancer cells. In many cases the recommended treatment is a radical prostatectomy. This entails surgically removing the *entire* prostate gland, as opposed to only that portion that obstructs urine flow in benign disease. When patients hear this, they assume they will end up permanently impotent. "You might as well cut off my penis!" they lament. But in most cases their fear is not justified.

As I mentioned earlier, the prostate is a secondary organ where sex is concerned. Your penis can perform perfectly well without it. Nevertheless, the old surgical cure for prostate cancer left 60 to 80 percent of patients impotent because it damaged the vital nerve bundles that make erection possible. Today we have developed a more precise *nerve-sparing* procedure, which has dramatically reduced the incidence of postoperative penis weakness. Approximately 80 percent of our patients emerge from their recuperation with their full penis power intact.

My first obligation, of course, is to do the best cancer operation I can. If the prostate tumor has extended to the adjacent nerve bundle, then I will cut the nerve bundle to remove the malignant tissue. As any sensible patient would agree, a surgeon's primary responsibility is to obliterate the cancer effectively. Sometimes, unfortunately, preserving the patient's life requires a sacrifice of penis power. I do everything possible to avoid that contingency, but when it is absolutely necessary we make the choice knowing that we can take further steps to help restore penis power.

A similar situation exists for other cancers in the genitourinary tract. Remarkable new technology enables us to diagnose cancer of the bladder and kidneys at an early stage and to treat those conditions in ways that preserve penis power. Even where the surgeon is forced to remove the bladder, prostate, vas deferens, and seminal vesicles all at once, the patient can still get an erection as long as that vital bundle of nerves is spared.

Testicular cancer, which affects mainly younger men, is relatively rare and is the most easily treated of all tumors in the genitourinary system. Just ten years ago, more than 90 percent of patients with certain types of testicular cancer did not survive five years; now the overwhelming majority are curable. In most cases where surgery is required we remove one of the two testes, since cancer rarely affects both at the same time. The surviving gonad will compensate by producing additional testosterone. And even if we have to remove both testes, we can preserve normal masculine functioning with testosterone injections or pills.

One last condition deserves mention. Unfortunately for patients who undergo kidney transplants, the penis power prognosis is not good. The main reason for this is that these patients usually have severe underlying disorders, such as advanced diabetes and/or extensive vascular or nerve disease. While my patients with only *one* kidney transplant often maintain penis power, those forced to undergo a second transplant typically report erection failure afterward because the blood supply that ordinarily serves the penis is "borrowed" for the newly transplanted kidney.

Also, many patients with kidney failure are on dialysis while they wait for an organ suitable for transplantation. During that phase I note that libido and sexual function usually decline. In addition, more than half of my patients on chronic dialysis develop penis weakness based on the ravages of their underlying disease, certain endocrine complications, and psychological despair.

THE GOOD NEWS

Now that we have examined the physical conditions that can diminish or destroy penis power, I must emphasize certain points. First, the disorders we discussed are not a death sentence to penis power. Only *some* diabetics, *some* men with nerve disease, *some* alcoholics, and *some* cancer patients become impotent. The conditions we discussed might produce only *partial* loss of penis power, or even none at all. And in many cases the impact on penis power can be reversed with medical treatment or lifestyle changes—by giving up destructive substances, for example, or controlling diabetes with diet and insulin, or improving blood flow with better nutrition, appropriate medication, and exercise.

Second, even with bona fide organic disorders, a significant portion of penis weakness is in the mind. Already saddened by the diagnosis of his disease, physically weak and emotionally vulnerable, a patient learns that men with his condition can suffer erection problems. The thought alone will weaken penis power in all but the most self-confident and upbeat of patients.

As with any setback, attitude is vital. A sick man with a positive mind-set will find ways to continue enjoying his sexuality to the maximum extent possible. Even if he has to stretch his imagination and alter his sex habits completely, even if he has to drastically limit his activities, a man with a superpotent attitude can retain his penis power regardless of his physical condition. I have had patients confined to wheelchairs who adapt to their circumstances and forge a new, superpotent way of life for themselves. Where there is penis power there is a way.

7

Medical Cures for Medical Problems

E ven for men with true physical loss of penis power, there is hope. Modern technology has been a tremendous boon, enabling us to help men with superpotent attitudes to function as normally as possible even with irreversible organic impotence. The progress in this area has been so remarkable that about three-quarters of what we can now do we could not have done five years ago. Let's look at some of our options.

SHOOTING IT UP

When the normal circulatory events that result in a good, firm erection cannot take place due to a physical disorder, we can produce instead a perfectly functional *pharmacological* erection. Our preferred method is to inject a medication into the shaft of the penis. The main drug used is prostaglandin E, a vasoactive substance that relaxes the smooth muscles in the walls of penile arteries, increasing blood flow into the corpora within the shaft through vessels that are partially blocked, usually by arteriosclerotic plaque. The results are dramatic. The penis becomes semierect within five to ten minutes and quite rigid in fifteen. In most instances, it remains erect for thirty to fifty minutes. Significantly, the drugs have no effect whatsoever on orgasm or ejaculation.

Since we began injecting these drugs safely a few years ago, we have restored thousands of penis-weakened men to an active, fulfilling sex life. After determining the proper drug and the precise dosage for each individual patient, we meticulously train him to inject himself. We use a tiny needle and a small syringe, similar to those used by a diabetic who self-injects insulin. Once we are satisfied that the patient has mastered the technique, we instruct him to inject the medication prior to intercourse. It is simple and painless, and the results are automatic; the injection will produce an erection even in an anesthetized patient. Interestingly, however, the effect can be modified by external stimuli. Erotic stimulation *enhances* the effect of the medication, probably because it increases the presence of the circulating neurotransmitters released by the brain when it is sexually aroused. These chemicals complement the dynamics of the drugs. By contrast, we have seen that the lack of privacy in the doctor's office can *reduce* the effect of the drugs. So the good news is, the drugs tend to work better in the bedroom than the examining room.

Needless to say, these drugs must not be used without strict medical supervision. Our instructions must be followed precisely, and active follow-up is essential. Moreover, because of possible side effects, certain men should not use injectable drugs: those with conditions such as varicose veins, where blood tends to pool; those with blood disorders such as sickle-cell anemia; those with unstable cardiovascular disease and symptoms such as fainting spells. And those whose limited dexterity or poor eyesight which could lead to errors when preparing the syringe or injecting the medication also should not use these drugs. Additionally, I am very cautious about prescribing this method for patients whom I consider emotionally unstable, as there is potential for misuse. In such cases, I strongly recommend psychological counseling before I administer the drugs.

One possible misuse of injectable drugs is to take them too

often. I am reminded of an extremely wealthy patient of mine, a man in his sixties with a history of superpotent activity. Needless to say, he reacted with great consternation when a vascular condition rendered him physically impotent, especially since he had recently married a world-class beauty two decades younger. I prescribed papaverine, determined the proper dosage, and taught him how to self-inject. He went off to his home in Europe and spent time with his wife on their yacht in the Mediterranean. From time to time he called to let me know that everything was great. When he returned to Los Angeles he came in for a checkup and raved about the therapy. He said he was having the best sex he'd had in thirty-five years—three times a day, sometimes for hours at a time.

He couldn't have been happier. And I couldn't have been more alarmed. I had specifically instructed him to inject the medicine no more than once every other day. I told him that what he was doing was dangerous. "How can it be dangerous?" he replied. "You always told me that sex is great exercise. I feel fabulous!"

That was not the point. I was concerned with the potential side effects of medically inducing erections six hours a day! The danger is a condition known as priapism—a painful, persistent erection that is not accompanied by sexual excitation. The problem is, if an erection lasts too long, the blood trapped in the penis does not drain. This can result in permanent damage to the delicate sinusoids within the penis, leading to impotence so severe that not even injectable drugs can counteract it.

Priapism is the most serious complication that can result from this form of therapy. It occurs very rarely, and almost always after the misuse of medication, but when it does happen we have to act quickly to avoid permanent damage. We instruct patients to phone us immediately if an erection lasts longer than two hours. If that should occur, the patient is instructed to come in immediately. We inject a Neo-Synephrine solution directly into the shaft of the penis to gradually reduce tumescence. In fact, we often give patients an emergency syringe with a proper dose of Neo-Synephrine, to be kept at home.

Other side effects that sometimes arise include dizziness, head-aches, a metallic taste in the mouth, bruising or inflammation of the penis, tingling sensations, and swelling or angulation after the injection. Most of these local complications are minor and can be avoided if the patient follows his instructions to the letter.

Those instructions, I should add, are extremely rigorous. The use of self-administered injections is one of those areas where "informed consent" is vital. My staff and I spend a great deal of time with the patient and his partner explaining the action of the drugs, the theory behind the therapy, the proper dosage and application, the risks and possible side effects. Each patient is also given a packet of printed material to take home with him.

One of the chief considerations for the urologist is to determine the proper dose. Not all men react the same way to a given dose of a vasoactive drug. We have to find the precise amount needed for that patient to achieve the goal: an erection that lasts thirty to forty-five minutes without side effects. The ideal dose varies, depending on the underlying cause of the problem, the patient's state of mind, and the psychological environment in which he takes it. Only after meticulously testing various doses in my office under controlled clinical conditions do I teach the patient to self-inject. We never allow a patient to administer drugs on his own until we are absolutely certain he has mastered all the necessary skills.

Patient response to the treatment varies. On one extreme are patients like the newly married European rich man who are so satisfied they abuse the privilege. On the other extreme are those who discontinue therapy, either because they are afraid of possible complications, they are squeamish about injecting themselves, or they are turned off by the loss of spontaneity caused by having to stop and inject the drug. The great majority fall in the middle, grateful for the medical technology that enables them to have a satisfying sex life and perhaps even achieve superpotency despite their medical limitations.

SURGICAL PROCEDURES

I am often asked if I can transplant penises the way I can kidneys. The answer is emphatically no. We can't electively transplant *any* appendage at this point, let alone one whose functions depend on such a complex mix of nerve, blood, and hormonal variables, all hinging on delicate feedback mechanisms. With all my faith in modern science, I cannot imagine a time when impotent men will be rejuvenated by the surgical transplant of real genitals. Even if the technology were possible, we have so many simpler alternatives I doubt it would ever be used.

Since many erection problems are caused by insufficient blood flow to the penis, medical science has naturally sought methods to reverse that problem. Studies so far have focused on ways to transfer blood from neighboring vessels to the deep arteries of the penis. These experiments, which are still in their infancy, have demonstrated some success in young men suffering from acute pelvic trauma. However, due to the complex vascular anatomy of the penis, we have so far been unable to duplicate the success we have had with coronary bypass surgery and the treatment of other arterial disorders. I predict that by the year 2000 surgical techniques will become applicable to many kinds of organic impotence caused by blood vessel obstruction.

Experimental work has also been done on the other side of the erection coin: preventing venous leaks. As I mentioned earlier, an erection can't be maintained unless the veins in the corpora hold in the blood. With modern diagnostic procedures we can tell when blood is leaving the venous channels in abnormal amounts. Although work in this area is still in its infancy, surgery can be performed on selected patients to impede the backflow of blood from the penis.

By far the most common surgical procedure for impotence is the implantation of a penile prosthesis. The combination of ingenious design, technical proficiency, and durability has made it possible to implant these prosthetics *directly* into the penis. Over the years, a variety of devices have been developed that can be easily implanted in an outpatient hospital setting. This has provided a permanent solution for thousands of organically impotent men who have a commitment to penis power and the motivation to undergo surgery. They allow for complete sexual satisfaction with a very low rate of failure. At one point in the late 1980s, about 30,000 prostheses were implanted each year around the world. Since the introduction of injectables, however, this number has declined dramatically.

There are basically two types of prostheses. The older variety is the so-called malleable implant, which consists of semirigid rods that are placed into the corpora (the bodies that normally fill with blood to create an erection), making the penis rigid enough to allow penetration. The problem with these devices is they don't change in length or girth, which means the man has to walk around with a semifirm penis at all times. The device is flexible enough to bend into a somewhat concealable shape, but the penis looks a bit unnatural and can be a source of some embarrassment at the health club.

The second type is the inflatable prosthesis. This consists of two inflatable cylinders that are surgically implanted in the same corporal channels, plus a pump and a fluid-filled reservoir usually implanted either within the scrotum or lower abdomen. When the patient desires an erection, he simply squeezes the pump several times and the fluid flows from the reservoir into the cylinders. The cylinders expand and swell, mimicking a natural erection. After intercourse, a release valve is simply pressed and the fluid flows back into the reservoir, returning the penis to its flaccid state.

Because this inflatable device allows the user full control and leaves the penis looking relatively normal, this type of implant is much preferred by my patients who consider prostheses. However, it requires a more extensive surgical procedure and has a higher rate of malfunction than malleable implants, which have no moving parts or connectors. Also, correcting mechanical failures is not like opening the hood of your car and replacing a spark plug; it requires another surgical incision.

In the past, the inflatable devices were frequently plagued by mechanical failures, often requiring repeat surgeries. The recent improvements by manufacturers have been dramatic, and the technology on the horizon promises to be even better. I predict that if inflatable prostheses continue to be profitable for manufacturers, the research and development dollars will be allocated and will lead to nonbreakable components that produce erections virtually indistinguishable from the real thing.

A word about my mind-set: before considering a patient for a prosthesis I meticulously rule out all *correctable* medical conditions. For me, implantation is the treatment of last resort. When the decision is made I inform the patient of the pros and cons of all the available devices. I still recommend the malleable device for many obese patients, for example. If the penis is partially hidden by a protruding belly, its artificial appearance is not as noticeable. With a slender man, however, the device stands out like the proverbial sore thumb. Once the choice is made, the device is implanted, usually under local anesthesia, with one cylinder placed in each corpora cavernosa. The surgical procedure takes about thirty to forty-five minutes. Complications during and after surgery are extremely rare, and postoperative discomfort is relatively short-lived. The body tolerates the implant almost as if it were made of flesh and blood.

It should be noted that each prosthesis is custom-fit for the patient; it has to be tailored to fit the precise length and width of the corpora. We cannot implant a prosthesis that is smaller, or the erections will have a floppy tip (the so-called SST Deformity, named for the droopy nose of the Concorde supersonic transport plane); nor can we implant a device that will make the penis longer, despite the fantasies of many patients. In other words, after a prosthesis, the functional penis, both erect and flaccid, will be the exact size it was before the implant.

The ideal candidate for a prosthesis is someone with all the mental characteristics of a superpotent man but who is unable to achieve a satisfactory erection because of a real medical disorder. I think, for example, of a patient of mine from a distant country whose culture is vastly different from our own. One of the wealthiest men in the world, he had been married for thirty-five years to a woman he loved and also had a concubine—an accepted custom in his society. This man had fathered approximately one child a year for nearly twenty years until he developed diabetes, which became so severe he was unable to have normal intercourse. After considering all his alternatives he opted for a penile prosthesis. Ever since the surgery, he and his loving wife (and concubine as well) have been grateful that the penis power that never left his heart was restored to the rest of him as well.

Thinking of that man's renewal, however, brings to mind another gentleman from that same part of the world, the prefect example of the *wrong* reason to have a prosthesis. A member of a royal family, he came to my office at age forty-two for a urologic problem unrelated to sexuality. When I examined him I noted that his penis looked truly ugly. He had a primitive prosthesis, which had been implanted years earlier, when he was only twenty-seven. At that time the available devices were crude even in America, and his had been implanted in a third world country that was hardly at the cutting edge of medical technology. Visually the result was grotesque.

He asked me if I could improve its appearance. I passed on the opportunity to perform what would essentially be cosmetic surgery, but I was curious as to *why* he had had the operation in the first place. He had no organic illness, yet this man, before he was even thirty, had chosen to endure the pain, embarrassment, and risk of having plastic implanted in his penis. His reasons were as repulsive as the prosthesis itself. It seems he was so rich he could have anything in the world. He had all the homes, boats, planes, cars, and toys a man could dream of. At the snap of his fingers, he could have an entourage of beautiful and willing women—and he snapped his fingers routinely when traveling outside his strict, conservative nation. He had everything money could buy, but the number and frequency of his erections were still limited by physiology. So he *bought* himself an unlimited erection. This was not a superpotent man. His warped view of the penis and its power represents the best possible reason for *not* having a penile prosthesis.

A more typical candidate, whom I routinely discourage from having an implant, is the eighty-year-old retired man who comes to me for a routine prostate exam and offers the news that he "can't get it up anymore." He wants a prosthesis like the one a friend of his has. The surgery had restored his friend's sex life, so why not his? Upon questioning, this scenario typically unfolds: he has been married for more than forty years to the same woman, and the marriage has brought him more aggravation than joy; he is in reasonably good health, but is often a sour, bitter man with very few interests and low self-esteem. He has, in effect, given up on life. There is nothing wrong with his sexual apparatus that a change in attitude and a renewed zest for life or a new partner would not cure. In such cases I advise *against* the implant.

Why refuse him when I had performed the operation on his friend? Because the friend was a man in his late seventies who had stayed involved in his business and enjoyed a variety of recreational activities. He was a spirited man, a widower with more than one younger girlfriend. He was a superpotent man whose penis power was not up to his penis demands due to a vascular problem that had also necessitated bypass surgery. This man was a perfect candidate for an implant; his friend was not.

MECHANICAL DEVICES

For impotent men who seek an alternative to surgery or self-injection, there are several other devices on the market. The most popular of these fit under the heading of "external vacuum therapy." Essentially, these gadgets produce erections by mimicking the physiology of oral sex. They use *suction*. First, a plastic cylinder is placed over the penis. A vacuum is then created, drawing blood into the penis and causing it to expand. When the penis becomes rigid enough for penetration— usually in a minute or two—the patient removes the cylinder and places a rubber band–like device around the base of his penis. The band impedes venous outflow so the erection can be maintained long enough for successful intercourse.

For the most part, I consider vacuum devices manufactured by reputable companies as safe. Among their advantages are low cost, little risk of side effects, and the avoidance of surgery, medication, or injections. The *disadvantages* are: They are awkward to handle and take a few minutes to assemble, thus reducing the pleasure and spontaneity of lovemaking; also, the ring can inhibit ejaculation in some patients.

As a whole, vacuum therapy is a reasonable alternative for many men, especially those who suffer from *partial* loss of erection and those who are unsure about having a prosthesis or injecting themselves with drugs. Professionally and personally, I would recommend good old-fashioned oral sex!

Mechanical devices should be used only under the supervision of a physician. I caution patients with blood disorders like sickle-cell disease or clotting problems not to use them. And they most certainly should not be used by healthy men who see them as easy ways to enhance their sexual performance. That would be the antithesis of true penis power.

APHRODISIACS AND OTHER SUBSTANCES

Virtually every culture in every period of history has a record of substances, primarily plants, alleged to stimulate sexual desire and improve virility. These range from the famous Spanish fly to complex combinations of Chinese herbs. Whether these substances actually work or their reported effects are attributable to the placebo effect I cannot say. I hasten to point out, however, that medical science has found very little evidence that aphrodisiacs work, and no ingestible substance has come to my attention that will cure penis weakness.

With the exception of hormones, the substance that has received the most press recently is *yohimbine*. Derived from the bark of the yohimbine tree, it has been considered an aphrodisiac by native cultures for hundreds of years, and initial studies beginning in 1978 have, to some degree, substantiated the claim. Dr. Christiaan Barnard, the eminent heart surgeon, used yohimbine on transplant patients who developed impotence and reported satisfactory results in 75 percent of his cases. Nonetheless, yohimbine therapy is not accepted by our mainstream medical community; we do not understand its biochemical action, and the original research was complicated by the fact that it was used in combination with other substances, such as testosterone.

More recently, in the mid-1980s, studies by reliable researchers have yielded provocative results. In a group of patients with organic impotence, about one-fifth reported a return to satisfactory sexual function after taking yohimbine. About the same number reported partial recovery, and the remainder reported no response at all. Patients identified as *psychologically* impotent reportedly had an even higher rate of improvement: about a third claimed to have recovered completely, and a third recovered partially, but the remaining third had no change at all.

Exactly to what extent yohimbine is effective, and for which men under which conditions, remains to be seen. But so far there is little reason for me to think that the bark can lend additional bite to men with penis weakness.

Another substance that holds promise is nitroglycerine, a potent relaxant of the smooth muscles lining the walls of all arteries. This drug has been used for many years in the treatment of angina pectoris, which is caused by decreased blood flow to the heart muscle, resulting in severe chest pain associated with exercise. Since nitroglycerine is effective when taken orally or as a paste or patch applied to the chest wall, early studies suggest that it might produce erections *without* the need to inject it directly into the penis. Theoretically, we should be able to apply nitroglycerine paste to the shaft of the penis and increase blood flow enough to produce better erections. These controlled studies showed a modest improvement in both the quality and quantity of erections. However, further research is needed before nitroglycerine can be considered a viable treatment for penis weakness.

Also, there is reason to wonder about possible side effects. One of my patients had to stop using the nitroglycerine paste when making love because the substance was absorbed by his wife's vaginal mucosa, giving her severe headaches. The same, by the way, might be true of minoxidil, a substance marketed as an aid to hair growth in balding men. Because it is a vasoactive substance, some people have suggested that rubbing it on the penis might produce better erections. I strongly urge you to refrain from self-experiments with such products until we know more about them. There are plenty of proven alternatives. Besides, who knows? You might grow hair on your penis!

I predict that the near future will see widespread use of safe, reliable pharmacological treatments for certain types of organic impotence. Whether that will entail yohimbine, nitroglycerine, minoxidil, or substances we have not yet discovered remains to be seen. My guess is that by the year 2000 patients will no longer use injections of vasoactive substances to induce erections, but will have oral and/or topical medications that produce the same vascular effects.

To summarize the message of this chapter, men who have a superpotent mind-set but are limited by illness or injury can reclaim their penis power with medical help. This is a magnificent advancement, one that promises even further strides in the near future. However, I must repeat that only a small percentage of men with penis problems have true organic impotence. The vast majority have normal, perfectly capable penises served by well-functioning auxiliary organs. There is nothing wrong with them physically. For these millions of men, surgery, drugs, and mechanical aids have no place. The answers for them lie between their ears.

8
When It's All in the Mind

Something's wrong with me, Doc," said Steve, a thirty-nine-year-old lawyer. "I want a complete urologic workup."

I asked him what the trouble was. "I met this great woman," he said. "We had a terrific time on our first date. She invited me in, one thing led to another, and before I knew it we were in bed. But I...well...I couldn't...you know..."

I knew all right. I had heard it so many times from hysterical patients. Steve was terrified that something had gone wrong with his penis. But his failure to get an erection with his terrific new woman had nothing to do with physiology. He had gone through a bitter divorce and it had taken some time to get used to being single again. The ill-fated date was the first time in many years that he had even kissed a woman in earnest other than his wife. Steve wasn't impotent, he was just plain nervous. The newness of the experience, the excitement of meeting someone he liked, and his eagerness to please her and prove himself a worthy bed partner, all conspired to create one of the greatest enemies of penis power: *anxiety*.

More penis weakness occurs the first time a man is with a particular woman than at any other time. And the sad thing is, when it happens, men feel so humiliated they sometimes find any excuse they can not to date the woman again, thereby depriving themselves of what might have been a good relationship. I've even met men who, after several embarrassments, stayed away entirely from women who turned them on. They became, in effect, celibate prisoners of penis performance anxiety.

It happens a lot with young guys. Take, for example, a college freshman named Clifford who was plagued by premature ejaculation and erection failure. In high school, when he was already uncertain of his masculinity and misled by the bravado of his buddies, Clifford's early sexual experiences were disasters. He kept trying, and because he was a handsome, rugged young man, he had no trouble finding girls. But when the sex didn't work out, he was so mortified he never tried it with the same girl a second time. And his *first* times got even worse because his performance anxiety increased with every bad memory. Eventually, he stopped dating altogether, except to escort girls to safe social events so he didn't have to go alone. In college, he created a fictitious out-of-town girlfriend so no one would get the wrong idea. But in fact Clifford was horny as a devil and sick and tired of masturbating, so he finally got up the nerve to tell me about his "mechanical problem."

His sexual self-esteem had taken such a beating he was convinced he needed medical help. After I examined him, we sat down in my office. "You don't have a mechanical problem, Cliff," I told him. "You have an attitude problem." I assured him that his early experience was not unusual. I told him that it's like getting back on a bicycle after you fall: you have to do it—in his case, preferably with the same bicycle. I encouraged him to find a girl he liked and stay with her long enough to feel calm and trusting when they were in bed. And, I added, if things don't go right the first time, don't panic. If the girl has a heart she'll understand, and next time you'll be much more relaxed.

Clifford was so relieved to hear he wasn't sick you'd have thought I had tested him for cancer. Sure enough, within weeks he fell in love with a sweet, understanding girl, and embarked on a steady, sexually satisfying relationship.

The first time with a new sexual partner can be the most exciting turn-on there is, but that very excitement can sometimes lead to temporary penis weakness, and we've already discussed how *one* bad experience can spiral into a pattern. It happens to a lot of kids like Clifford, and to grown men who have been out of circulation like Steve. In Steve's case, the same advice applied: take your time, be patient, stop pressuring yourself, stop thinking you're inadequate, and find a partner who makes you feel comfortable and unthreatened. It worked for him, and it will work for you too if that's what you're going through.

The point of these stories is not just that first encounters can be as traumatic as they are exciting; there are lots of other reasons for temporary penis weakness as well, but I want to start by discussing *performance anxiety*. In my experience, that is the leading cause of penis failure, and it's much more likely to happen when you're with an unfamiliar partner or when you feel pressured to measure up to some standard.

The main point is, what you think is a *physical* problem is probably all in your mind. Chances are the cause is something simple and obvious, like ordinary, common, run-of-the-mill performance anxiety, or something else that can be fixed with a change of perspective or a change of circumstances. If you let anxiety get the best of you, you'll be making a molehill out of a mountain. That is, instead of a mountainous erection, you'll end up with a flaccid molehill because of fears that are unworthy of you.

Don't let a single disappointment convince you that you are less than a man or that something is wrong with your penis. Losing an erection once in a while is as much a part of sex as booting a ground ball is to a shortstop or missing a target is to a marksman. When it happens, move on. If you hold on to the memory of failure it will surely become the seed of future failures. If a shortstop were to think about his previous mistakes every time he stepped on the field, you know what the result would be: before long he'd be leading the league in errors.

ACCENTUATE THE POSITIVE

Take a lesson from successful men in other fields. When I meet men in leadership positions, I observe that they never think in terms of failure. They don't even use the term. They prefer "mistake," or "error," or "setback," because the F word implies a certain finality or permanency that they just don't accept. Successful people focus on positive goals. They put all their energy into the task at hand. They don't look back, they don't make excuses, and they are not intimidated by setbacks. If things don't go well, they analyze the situation and use the lessons they learn to carve out subsequent triumphs.

Of course, you have to learn the *right* lessons from your setbacks. That was precisely the problem with Clifford and Steve. They drew the *wrong* conclusions. The lesson they came away with was, "There's something wrong with me." Clearly, that is not the attitude of a successful man in any field, and it is not the attitude that will fortify your penis power.

Management expert Warren Bennis coined a term that captures the superpotent attitude as it relates to performance anxiety: the "Wallenda Factor." He named it after Karl Wallenda, the world famous aerialist. When Wallenda stepped out on a tightrope with nothing but air between him and the ground, he never thought of failure. He was fearless, seemingly impervious to the danger of falling. He did not even think of *not* falling or *not* embarrassing himself. His full attention was on what he had to do at that moment. Unfortunately, while Wallenda's career illustrates the importance of having the right attitude, his ultimate fate demonstrates what can happen if you do not.

In 1978, before walking a tightrope seventy-five feet above the ground, Wallenda was different for some inexplicable reason. According to his wife, "All Karl thought about for three straight months prior to it was *falling*. It was the first time he'd ever thought about that, and it seemed to me that he put all his energies into *not falling* rather than walking the tightrope." For the first time, he personally supervised the installation of the rope and checked to see that the guy wires were secure. It is believed that, because of his preoccupation with falling, the great Wallenda fell to his death.

Which is, metaphorically speaking, exactly what Clifford and Steve and millions of other men do when they approach sex with their minds consumed by the fear of failure. You end up defining your goal as not embarrassing yourself rather than having a good time and extracting the maximum pleasure for you and your partner. Take a lesson from Wallenda: don't think about falling, don't think about past setbacks, don't think about anything other than the task at hand. Put your attention completely on the sensual experience of lovemaking.

What can you do if you *do* have performance anxiety? Let's start with the anticipation of using your penis. When you begin to feel anxious or fearful, you must realize that you are programming your mind for failure. Stop what you're doing, calm yourself down, and remind yourself that "you have nothing to fear but fear itself." What is the worst thing that could happen? You'll embarrass yourself? Well, you can only be embarrassed if you let yourself be. If you think that a "real man" can't possibly lose an erection or come too quickly, then you'll be embarrassed if those things happen. But if you know in your heart and mind that such things happen to *every* real man at some time, you won't be all that embarrassed if it happens. And what if you *are* embarrassed? How bad is that really? Keep in mind that the worst thing you can possibly anticipate is not really all that big a deal. This will help you stay calm and lighthearted, and if you feel that way your penis is likely to behave itself. If you develop the ability to laugh at yourself and that unpredictable appendage of yours, it will do you wonders.

Get rid of fearful, negative thoughts altogether. There is no valid reason to entertain them. They are the natural enemy of your penis. Mobilize a battalion of *positive* thoughts and let them take over your mind. One thing I tell my patients to do is stand before a mirror, naked. Look at your penis. Talk to it. Stroke it fondly. Tell it you have confidence in it. Tell it you know it's a normal, healthy organ with all its vessels, nerves, and channels in perfect working order. Tell it if it malfunctioned in the past it was all your fault for sending it nervous, frightened signals. Tell it you'll try not to do that anymore. Tell it you have every intention of adopting the thoughts and attitudes of a superpotent man. This might sound ridiculous or childish, but I promise you it works. *Penis power is nothing more than the power of positive thinking applied to your penis.*

Now, I have had patients report back to me and say, "Well, Doctor, I did what you said and I was *still* nervous." Sometimes the fear is so deep-rooted that you can't bring yourself to believe your own pep talk. As you fill your brain with positive thoughts, another part of your brain is snidely whispering, "Bullshit!" My advice is, keep those positive thoughts coming. Keep the pep talks coming. Work at it relentlessly. In the long run, even the most cynical disbeliever—yourself—will be convinced, and that conviction will manifest in positive penis behavior.

I'm fully aware of the fact that some men with deep, powerful fear of penis failure need more than a pep talk. In such cases, I recommend that they talk to a psychotherapist and explore the deeper reasons for their anxieties. In almost every case, however, such people are desperately lacking in basic self-esteem, not just fear of penis failure. They think so poorly of themselves, their image of themselves as men is so low, that it affects every aspect of their lives, not just sex. However, it is far easier to compensate for low self-esteem in business or sports, for example, than it is in bed. Lots of men who are plagued by self-doubt are extremely successful professionally. But *your penis never lies, and your penis is never fooled.* It is a perfect reflection of your deepest thoughts and emotions. So even if you *think* you have no self-esteem problem, even if you tell yourself that you're a pretty terrific guy, if you worry about your sexual performance you can bet that some part of you has serious doubts about your masculinity. And self-doubt travels from the brain to the penis in a flash.

You might have to work on your basic self-esteem, either

with the help of a counselor or on your own. If you're not sure if you have a self-doubt problem, ask yourself some questions: Do you constantly compare yourself to other men? When something minor goes wrong, do you scold yourself or call yourself insulting names? Do you judge yourself more harshly than you judge others? Do you find yourself trying hard to please other people or to be liked by everyone? Are you overly sensitive to the criticism of others? When you do something well, do you belittle your accomplishment? Do you have a strong need to prove yourself? When faced with a new challenge do you immediately worry that you won't measure up?

If you answered yes to most of those questions, chances are you have a deep-seated tendency to doubt yourself and assess yourself harshly. And if that's the case, your penis is picking up on your lack of self-acceptance. If *you* don't think you're capable of good, solid penis performance, why should your penis act otherwise? If *you* don't think you deserve a fully satisfying sex life, why should your penis give one to you?

You should be doing everything in your power to raise your self-esteem. Look at all the positive things you've accomplished. Look at all the kind, generous things you do. Look at all your admirable traits. Examine the standards by which you measure yourself. Self-doubt comes from the failure to live up to what you expect of yourself, and if what you expect is based on standards that are imposed by other people, social institutions, or the media, then you're not being true to yourself. Who says you're supposed to live up to some arbitrary standard? Who says you're less of a man if you don't? *Set your own penis standards and then evaluate yourself with generosity.*

LIGHTEN UP, DUDE

All right, you're in bed with a sexy woman, whether it's your wife of thirty years or someone you just met. You feel tense. You start to worry that it won't get hard, or that you might lose the "boner" that just popped up. What do you do? The usual reaction is panic. You start to worry so much about your penis that you tense up. You get clumsy. You try to exert willpower on your organ. You forget all about doing the things that turn on your partner. You can't appreciate, or even feel, the kisses and strokes she is so lovingly giving you. One of two things is bound to happen next: your woman gets turned off and thinks she's doing something wrong; or your penis goes limp. From my observations, usually both.

So, what should you do about it? The minute you start to feel any anxiety, stop what you're doing immediately and *tell* your partner about it. Don't make excuses. Don't try to hide it. Own up to it. Tell her candidly that you're nervous. Explain that this sometimes happens to you—as, I assure you, it does to all men. Tell her it's because you want so much to give her pleasure and satisfaction, and because her acceptance means a lot to you. Make sure she understands that it's not her fault, that she's terrific, that she hasn't done anything wrong. Tell her it's all in your head and it will surely go away.

Honesty is always the best policy in general, but especially when it comes to your penis. Ninety-nine percent of the time candor will improve the situation by defusing the tension. If you have a good relationship, your partner will understand. She will appreciate your integrity and your vulnerability. Most women want intimacy, affection, and closeness in bed, so if you communicate those qualities she will not hold your anxiety against you. She will probably reassure you, calm you down, and take the pressure off. The result will be a resurgence of your penis power. If she does *not* act this way, if she gets angry or resentful, if she cuts you down in a castrating way... well, maybe you should ask yourself if you're in bed with the right woman.

And if you *do* fail to get an erection? If you *do* lose it at precisely the wrong moment? If you *do* ejaculate too quickly? What then? Laugh it off! Sure, you must be thinking, easy for the doctor to say. But I mean it. Joke about it. Lighten up! I assure you, "real men" can laugh at their own penises. "Oh, well, that rascal pulled a fast one on me. Can't get him to behave sometimes. Unpredictable little devil. Don't take it personally. Remarks like that, expressed in your own words and your own style, should ease the tension and help your penis rise another day, or even the same day. Medically speaking, I can practically guarantee it.

More than likely, your partner will appreciate the light touch. She might be thinking there's something wrong with *her*. She might be feeling guilty for failing you. She might know that you feel ashamed but not know quite what to say or do about it. You can take the lead and break the ice with a good chuckle. Who says sex has to be so serious? When you get right down to it, with all the unstated agendas, the physical clumsiness, the childlike awkwardness, and so forth, sex is just as well suited for slapstick comedy as fine art or soft-focus cinematography. In fact, many people say that there is no better turn-on than a good hearty laugh in bed, and nothing sexier than a partner whose sense of humor is compatible with your own. Just don't take your penis so damn seriously. That's how the trouble started in the first place.

And if you don't succeed, try, try again. And again, and again. Don't shy away from using your penis if it falls down on the job once or twice—or any number of times. Don't give up on it. Practice makes perfect in sex just as it does elsewhere. Perseverance is the only way to get over setbacks and gain the confidence you need to overcome your fear of failure.

I think of a former patient of mine whom I'll call Joe. A short man with a classic Napoleonic complex, Joe had gone from one business to another, becoming fabulously successful in each before moving on to the next challenge. A bachelor at forty, he talked so much about the women he dated that I assumed he was having a healthy, varied sex life. To my astonishment, this human dynamo was plagued by penis weakness. It stemmed from deep deficiencies in self-esteem. All his accomplishments, it turned out, were a futile, workaholic attempt to gain the approval he never got from his father, a domineering man who raised his son like the Great Santini did his. Inside, Joe saw himself as worthless. When he was alone with a woman he perspired from fear, not passion, and 90 percent of the time his performance was the equivalent of bankruptcy.

But Joe had one thing going for him: perseverance. In everything he did, this was a determined, never-say-die man. Once he finally owned up to his dissatisfaction with his penis performance he applied to the boudoir the same determination he brought to business. A therapist helped him deal with his self-esteem problem and I thoroughly evaluated his urologic apparatus and assured him that he was fully capable of attaining penis power. Soon he was a more contented person with a fulfilling sexual relationship.

Joe is a stark contrast with another patient I'll call Daniel. Daniel also suffered from crippling self-doubt and penis weakness, only he expressed it in the opposite way. He was a classic underachiever in all aspects of his life, including sex. An outstanding guitarist, he had been a child prodigy in music as well as an A student. But his low self-esteem kept him from realizing his potential, just as it prevented him from making the most of his appealing looks and likable, self-effacing personality. At twenty-nine, he eked out a living teaching guitar, and he spent every night alone. When I met him, Daniel hadn't had a date in over a year. A series of disappointing experiences had relegated sex and romance to the realm of pure fantasy. Daniel lacked what Joe had: perseverance and the courage to expose himself to possible failure in order to conquer his fear. He is still wrestling with his self-doubt and trying to build up the courage to try again, just like a little kid who is too scared to get back on his bicycle after taking a spill.

Perseverance is a good way to succeed at anything worthwhile. Among the most successful people in history are those who have the will to stick it out when others would have given up the fight. Whenever I think of perseverance I think of a certain country lawyer who lost his job, lost an election for the state legislature, failed in private business, failed to land a nomination for Congress, and was twice defeated for the Senate. All this while persevering enough to earn some victories and end up our most revered president. So, the next time you're ready to give up on your penis, think of Abraham Lincoln.

However, I must add a caveat to that advice: *persevere, but don't try too hard.* If you do, you just might make things worse. Joe, my Napoleonic patient, was one of those guys who approached every task with a full frontal assault. That's how he went about building his penis power. The trouble is, becoming superpotent is not like making a better business deal or improving your tennis game. Some tasks succeed because of hard work and effort. But getting an erection is not one of them; the more you work at it the less likely you are to succeed. It's analogous to falling asleep. Anyone who has ever tossed and turned with insomnia can tell you that the harder you *try* to sleep the more agitated you get and the longer you stay awake.

It's what I call the *Penis Paradox:* the harder you try, the softer it gets. You can't *will* your penis to get hard or stay hard; you can't implore it, order it, command it, or force it. The anxiety of trying to get an erection works against the natural process of getting one. As with sleep, you just have to create the right conditions and stay out of the way. Joe actually had *more* problems the minute he decided to conquer his penis weakness, because he tried so hard to perform well he couldn't possibly relax enough to get an erection. Only when he learned to calm down and let go, to simply enjoy what he was doing and let nature take its course, did things get better. From that point on his perseverance began to pay quick dividends.

The bottom line is, your penis *wants* to get hard. That's what it does. That is its nature, just as your heart wants to beat, your lungs want to breathe, your stomach wants to digest. They are all involuntary functions. So is getting an erection. Believe in your penis. Trust it. Give it every opportunity to do its job. But give it the freedom you would give a trusted friend or colleague to carry out his responsibilities. Just stay out of its way.

DON'T WORRY, BE SUPERPOTENT

Anxiety in any shape or form is the worst enemy of your penis. And I don't just mean anxiety about your performance. If you're nervous about finances, or the health of a loved one, or your kid's college application, or some business situation, or any of a myriad of things, your penis might let you down even if you have great faith in it. Worries and fears are physically debilitating. They cause wear and tear to the endocrine and nervous systems, and to the blood vessels, so how can they not affect your penis?

Don't let worry and fear into your bedroom! Park your anxieties at the threshold. In fact, park them out on the street. Don't let them anywhere near where you make love.

The trick is to learn how to *compartmentalize*. My most well-rounded, superpotent patients come by this skill naturally. Business is business, play is play, family is family, religion is religion, sex is sex. They don't mix things up in practice or in their minds. No matter how stressful things are at the office, the minute they leave the building they leave the stress behind. They never let it pollute their family lives or their sexual performance. If their kids are goofing off at school, if their roof is leaking, if their in-laws are hounding them, if their mechanic said fixing the car will cost a small fortune, or whatever, they leave those domestic hassles outside the bedroom door. Of course, that is easier said than done if the problems are between the two sex partners, but we'll deal with that issue later.

If you find it difficult to compartmentalize, you'll have to work at it. Anytime irrelevant, negative thoughts intrude on your penis performance, push them aside, send them away, tell them to get lost, and shift your attention to the erotic sensations you're experiencing as you make love. For some people, shifting attention is as easy as switching channels on a TV. Others need to work at it the same way they have to work at changing any old habit—and negative thinking is often just that, *a habit*. A psychologist colleague of mine recommends a visualization exercise to help you out. In your mind's eye, see yourself gathering up your troubles and placing them in a box. Then watch yourself seal the box and put it outside the door or toss it out the window. Get those worries out of the bedroom and give your penis permission to do its thing without interference. For the most part, worry, like anger and anxiety, are nonproductive emotions, particularly when it comes to penis performance.

Nothing is worth the price of worry, especially something as vital and pleasurable as penis power. My advice is, cultivate what Bertrand Russell called "the habit of thinking of things at the right time." The bedroom is not the place for planning next week's schedule, or rehearsing a speech in your mind, or worrying about tomorrow's board meeting—especially if you're concerned about something over which you have no control. "The wise man thinks about his troubles only when there is some purpose in doing so," wrote Russell. "At other times he thinks about other things, or, if at night, about nothing at all." He was referring to sleep, but if you want to be a superpotent man, apply it to penis activities as well.

One way to help keep anxious, worrisome feelings from inhibiting your penis power is to burn off some of your stress beforehand. Volumes have been written about neutralizing the effects of stress, so there is no need to take up space here with the rationale for this advice. Suffice to say that it might make it easier to compartmentalize if, before you get intimate with your lover, you lift some weights, run a few miles, swim a few laps, play racquetball, take a yoga class, pound a punching bag, walk on the beach, or whatever suits you. Take advantage of any way you can think of to burn off stress before you get into bed.

Or burn it off *in* bed. That's right: the best way I know to get rid of stress is to have sex. Here we have another Penis Paradox: stress can interfere with penis power, but at the same time *exercising* your penis power is a terrific way to burn off stress. I can't count the number of superpotent men who have told me that their favorite antidote for their high-pressured professional lives is to hurry home to their wife or girlfriend. It's a great physical exercise, it's a great way to release tension, it's wonderful for clearing the mind, and it has fringe benefits that other activities can't approach, like sharing affection and intimacy and feeling good about yourself. If you can learn to channel your frustration, anger, and worries into sexual energy you can turn the tables on stress. This is what performers do; instead of letting anxiety debilitate them, they use it as an energizer and a motivator. They channel it into their performances. So don't let anxiety diminish your penis power; use it to *boost* your penis power.

I once said exactly that to a talent agent whose workday was like a dream cooked up by the phone company and the makers of ulcer medication: one high-pressure phone call after another. It was destroying his penis power because he did not have the ability to compartmentalize. "Don't wait till after supper and the kids go to sleep and you're passing out on your feet," I told him. "Grab your wife and go to bed when you get home and burn off that stress before it burns you."

A week later he told me he couldn't do it. Why? Because he felt guilty. He thought his wife would feel he was using her, that he was having sex with her to satisfy his own physical needs, not because he wanted to share the joy of lovemaking with her. This was a noble thought from a man who truly loved his wife, but it was also irrational. He was having penis problems anyway, thanks to all that stress. Knowing his wife, I urged him to follow my advice despite his reservations. My hunch proved correct: his wife not only thought hopping into bed for a quick aggressive workout was romantic, but was only too happy to help her husband burn off the stress so he didn't carry it around with him all night.

If you have a good, loving relationship, your partner will not feel exploited if you use sex to combat stress. Believe me, she'll prefer to see you calm and collected rather than nervous and worried. If you take care of her needs at the same time you're satisfying your own penis, you will both end up winners.

DEPRESSION DEPRESSES THE PENIS

Another of the many patients who have come to me thinking they were penis failures was a sweet, gentle man named Bill, who worked at my hospital as an orderly. A divorced father of three, he had suddenly developed a bad case of penis weakness after two years of a healthy sex life with his girlfriend. It didn't take long to figure out why. In taking a routine medical history, I found out he had also been sleeping badly and losing weight. When I asked about his state of mind, Bill replied that he'd been depressed lately. It turned out that his son was addicted to cocaine and had been caught stealing to support his habit. In addition to the deep sadness anyone would feel over this misfortune, Bill was plagued by feelings of helplessness and remorse.

Needless to say, there was nothing wrong with Bill's sexual apparatus. His penis power hadn't disappeared. It was just on hiatus because of *situational depression*. Loss of interest in sex is a common, predictable response to deep sadness or personal loss. Bill hadn't been feeling like having sex at all, but instead of just accepting that and letting time take its course, he made things worse by forcing himself to sleep with his girlfriend. He was afraid she would think less of him if he said he didn't feel like making love. He also thought it would make him less of a man, and his manhood had just taken a beating because he blamed his son's problem on his own shortcomings as a father. So he went about lovemaking on schedule, but he couldn't lie to his penis: it wasn't ready to perform, because Bill's sexual energy had gone into a slump along with his appetite and his zest for playing softball.

Depression is a serious obstacle to superpotency. In Bill's case it was a temporary condition brought on by an identifiable situation. Once he understood what was going on and was able to accept the fact that his condition was normal, he was fine. In time, he got over the pain, the sadness dissipated, and life—including his penis—returned to normal.

In other cases, depression can be a chronic, debilitating disease and its effect on penis power can be long-lasting. Such conditions are beyond the scope of a urologist. If you have penis weakness because you suffer from chronic depression, it would be a mistake to focus on your sexuality alone. Your penis problem is one of many predictable symptoms. I urge you to see a psychiatrist who can diagnose and treat your condition properly. Today, medication, psychotherapy, or a combination of both can effectively manage the depression, and with the overall improvement of the condition comes a natural restoration of penis power.

MIND GAMES

Martin was a middle-aged man who had lost his wife, the love of his life, a year before he came to see me. After what he considered an appropriate period of mourning, he had begun to say yes when friends offered to set him up with dates. His first few were with sexually liberated women, and things went very well for Martin, considering that his only sexual experiences outside of marriage had been some furtive encounters with prostitutes when he was a very young man. But finally, when he met someone he really cared for, he suddenly lost his penis power. He couldn't understand it. Why should he perform well with women he felt indifferent about and might never see again, but not with someone he truly liked?

It turned out that Martin was plagued by *guilt*. He had no trouble with the first few women because he knew nothing would come of the relationships. They were there purely for fun and to ward off loneliness. But when he met someone he truly wanted to be with and the sex became more intimate and loving, he was overwhelmed by the thought that he was betraying his late wife. To spare himself the guilt feelings, his mind "tricked" his penis into falling down on the job.

Martin's case is one example of how penis power can be undermined by irrational emotions. Guilt is a big one, of course, and the biggest factor in that department is religion. I have known many Christians, Jews, and Muslims who were perfectly fine within the prescribed context of marriage but were driven to penis weakness when they indulged in behavior that overstepped the boundaries of their religious precepts. It is not my role to question anyone's religious beliefs. However, I will say that anyone who chooses to violate them should understand what his subconscious shame might do to his penis. In most cases they need to talk to a clergyman, not a urologist.

Another obstacle to penis power is *irrational* fear. I'm not referring to fear of performance failure or other actual threats, but the bizarre fear of dire consequence if one engages in intercourse. For example, I remember one thirty-year-old man who would have been a virgin had it not been for one woman who coaxed his semierect penis into her vagina. Every other experience ended in erection failure or ejaculation before penetration. I referred him to a psychotherapist, who discovered that this poor soul was raised by a domineering mother who told him as a young boy that vaginas had teeth! He had nightmares about getting it "chewed up."

That patient was an extreme case, but there are many men who fear intercourse for reasons they don't quite understand. In fact, many don't even realize that they are afraid. They think they want to have sex, they seek it out, but something always goes wrong and they conclude that their penises are abnormal. Whether it is the wrath of God, the spirit of their mothers, or vaginal teeth, some deep fear renders their penises weak.

A major factor, of course, is the fear of disease. I have many patients whose penises failed them because they were afraid of getting a heart attack during sex or of catching some highly unlikely disease like typhoid. These are bizarre terrors rooted in some deeper fear of sex. But other worries, I'm sorry to say, are not entirely irrational. There is very good reason to be concerned about sexually transmitted diseases nowadays, whether viral infections such as herpes, bacterial infections like syphilis and gonorrhea, or the elusive chlamydia organism—all of which have been on the increase in recent years—or AIDS. Needless to say, while the others can cause suffering and inhibit your sex life, AIDS has become the principal pariah because it alone is both incurable and deadly. Fear of AIDS has put a crimp in the lives of many of my patients who are superpotent men—as well it should.

But the time to worry about disease is not at the moment of intercourse. You should think that through long before you get into bed with someone. In today's world, it behooves a superpotent man to get to know a potential sex partner as well as possible. You must have the patience and courage to ask probing questions about her past sexual practices and part-ners. You might have to delay gratification, but you could be saving your life. If you take sound medical precautions, engage only in safe practices, and exercise sensible penis judgment, you should be free of fear when it's time to unleash your penis power.

9

Extenuating Circumstances

Larry was a fifty-one-year-old man who came to me for a prostate exam. When I informed him that his prostate was indeed enlarged and would require treatment, possibly even surgery, his response was amazing: he was relieved. I asked him why he was so happy to hear he had a prostate disorder. "Because, I've been having problems getting hard lately, Doc," he confessed. "I thought maybe I'd become impotent, so I'm glad to know it's only a minor prostate problem."

"Larry," I said, "I'm sorry to have to tell you this, but your prostate has nothing to do with it. If you're having problems with your penis, the surgery is not going to change anything." As I explained earlier, the prostate's role is to supply seminal fluid; it is not related to penis power.

Now he was really depressed. We had a long talk about his medical history and his personal life. Larry had been married to the same woman for nearly thirty years. Thirty years of ups and downs, of raising children and dealing with hassles day in and day out, of watching each other sag and wrinkle, of routine, habitual sex. Larry was not impotent. There was nothing wrong with him physically. He was suffering from nothing more than the Coolidge Effect.

The Coolidge Effect was named by researchers in animal

sexuality, but I think you will easily see the relevance for human beings. If you put a male animal in a cage with a female in heat, he will quickly mount her. After he ejaculates, he will rest before going at it again. The time he takes to rejuvenate—the refractory period—is predictable. It varies from one species to another, but it is consistent among all rats, roosters, rams, or whatever. After the second ejaculation, the male will rest again, only this time the refractory period is longer. The same is true after the third copulation, the fourth, fifth, and so on. The animal takes longer and longer to recover, until he finally reaches exhaustion.

That much seems obvious. Now here is the interesting part. If at any point you remove the female and replace her with a new one, all bets are off. It's back to square one for the male. No matter how many times he's ejaculated, introduce a new female and his refractory period bounces back to what it might have been after one or two copulations. This is the Coolidge Effect.

Why that name? Well, the story has it that President Calvin Coolidge, the austere conservative they called Silent Cal, was visiting a farm with his wife. Noticing an unusually large number of chicks and eggs, Mrs. Coolidge remarked that the few roosters in the barnyard must be prodigious studs. The farmer replied, proudly, that the roosters did their duty dozens of times a day. "You might point that out to Mr. Coolidge," said the First Lady.

Evidently, Silent Cal was not as prudish as his reputation suggests. He asked the farmer if each rooster had to service the same old hen every time. When the farmer told him that the roosters could mate freely with any hen they wanted to, the President responded, "You might point that out to Mrs. Coolidge."

No one is quite sure if that story is true, but if it's not it *should* be, and it deserved to have an effect named after it.

I have seen Larry's problem in hundreds of men. They think there is something wrong with them, but what's wrong is a matter of circumstances, not their penises. Sometimes the situations that cause temporary penis weakness are so obvious you would think the man himself would recognize it and save the time and expense of seeing a urologist. But men are so vulnerable to self-doubt in that area that they immediately think there is something wrong with their anatomy.

One of the most common of these circumstances is what Larry described to me: the inevitable boredom and habituation between long-term partners. Things become routine after a while. The thrill of taking off a woman's clothes is not so thrilling when you've unveiled the same body hundreds of times and it parades before you naked every day of your life (one survey found that 51 percent of men fantasize about someone else during sex, while only 37 percent of women do). If your wife of twenty plus years says she wants you, it's not quite the same turn-on as having the same words whispered into your ear by a shapely stranger. And let's be honest: you don't have to be youth-obsessed or an ageist to be more turned on by a young, tight, lithe body than the familiar one that gravity and time have altered. Nor do you have to be sexist; I'd wager that the same holds true for women, although perhaps not to the same degree.

There is no question that *new equals exciting*, whether it's a new car, a new song, or a new sex partner. Nothing will revive a man more quickly and more vigorously than a new woman, preferably a young, attractive woman who is turned on by him. That might sound subversive to those who value monogamy and those who cherish the undeniable spiritual and emotional benefits of lasting love. Nevertheless, when it comes to penis power, I've seen the evidence thousands of times over: men who have trouble making love to their wives can be dynamos with their mistresses; men can be troubled by penis problems until they get divorced and suddenly find rejuvenation with a new lover.

Now I'm not suggesting that the French have it right by condoning the tradition of mistresses. It is not my place to endorse any particular lifestyle. What I'm saying is, penis weakness is often circumstantial, and one of the primary circumstances is defined by the Coolidge Effect. An awful lot of men, especially middle-aged men, think they're losing their potency, when the only thing that's happening is a predictable lessening of desire due to a sex life built around monotonous routine. For some men, the solution just might be a mistress or a fling, if for no other reason than to restore their faith in their penises.

However, I hasten to warn men who assume that what's new is better that thinking that way can be dangerous. I have seen too many men jeopardize, and sometimes forfeit, long-standing relationships of immense value because they followed their penises in pursuit of something new and young. In many instances, they merely substitute one set of problems for another. They solve their boredom problem temporarily, only to realize they desperately miss the love, companionship, and other advantages that they squandered. Their penises are reborn temporarily, only to retreat again when their new, exciting lives grow stale. So beware of the *hard dick syndrome*! After a while it can turn into the Coolidge Effect.

Solutions to the Coolidge Effect can often be found within the confines of a good monogamous relationship. Those same animal researchers found that the male's vigor can return even without a new female if something else is altered, such as the scent or appearance of the old familiar mate. Obviously, there is a lesson here for humans, male and female. Like anything else, sex can settle into a dull routine. Familiarity might not breed contempt, but it certainly breeds boredom and disinterest. Break your habits. Change your routines. Use your imagination. Do it in different places. Do it at different times. Wear different clothing. Daub yourselves with unusual scents. Try different positions. Experiment with different types of foreplay. Whatever it takes to bring a sense of freshness and adventure to your sex life, do it. Just don't give up on yourself thinking you're over the hill or that you suddenly became impotent.

Problems that stem from longevity and familiarity might seem to contradict something we talked about in the previous chapter: first encounters of the close kind. Am I saying that being with a hot new woman for the first time can cause temporary penis failure, and so can being with the same woman for a long period of time? Yes. This is another Penis Paradox. Either set of circumstances can cause problems, but for very different reasons. First-time problems arise because it is *too* exciting. The anticipation, the apprehension, the anxiety over your performance, all are heightened in a new encounter, and that can cause you to lose an erection or ejaculate too quickly.

With a longtime partner the problem is exactly the opposite, as anyone who has ever been married will testify. The problem arises not because of anxiety or first-time jitters but because of diminished desire. When you've been with someone many times, it simply takes more time and more direct stimulation to get aroused. If you don't take that into consideration and add some spice and imagination to the routine, you might find that your penis is going, "Ho hum, I can't get worked up over this." If you're just going through the motions, it might just lie down on the job.

So we have two sets of circumstances, one diametrically opposed to the other, both of which can cause temporary penis weakness. The solution to first-time anxiety is to cultivate a comfortable, relaxed, familiar relationship. But if *that* reaches a critical mass and the problem of monotony sets in, the antidote is to generate excitement with freshness and variety.

THE SPICE OF LIFE

As a urologist, I can't emphasize this point enough: do everything in your power to prevent sex from becoming a dull routine. Nothing will bring passion and romance back to a long-term relationship faster than a change in sexual practice and venue. I remember one fifty-five-year-old patient who was married to a woman he loved for twenty-seven years. He had a bad case of sexual ennui, which led to a brief fling with his dentist's assistant. That, in turn, made things even worse at home because now he was inhibited by guilt in addition to boredom. I told him, "Jack, take Friday off, get your wife to cancel all her plans, and rent a cabin in the mountains for the weekend. You haven't done anything spontaneous and romantic in years. Do it. Tune out the world. No kids, no phone, no TV, just the two of you and a fireplace."

The weekend rejuvenated Jack and his wife, as have similar escapes for uncountable numbers of couples. In other cases, I've advised patients to take the afternoon off and surprise their wives with flowers and an afternoon tryst in a motel. Other couples have done things like pretend they've just met and are having a one-night stand. Or they simply vary their rituals. If you've been initiating sex after you're both washed and undressed and in bed, try doing it before all those bedtime rituals. When was the last time you and your wife undressed each other, instead of starting out in your pajamas? When was the last time you necked in the living room and carried her into the bedroom? Or made love in the kitchen? Have you tried a different position anytime in the last few years? Have you thought of using props? Go browse in a sex shop and see what you come up with (but stay away from the whips and chains). Above all, use your imagination. That's what it's there for.

Chances are you won't have to go extremes, like the wife in that Woody Allen movie who could only get turned on in public places. But if you simply give yourself permission to break your boundaries, you'll find your penis power jacked up several notches. You might have to do some cajoling to win your partner's support, but that can be a turn-on in itself.

Some of my patients just had to be told that it's okay to have sex at different times of day. Sex is not just a nighttime activity. Why do something that important when you're at your lowest energy level? Maybe your penis problem is really a fatigue problem. We don't know enough to say that the penis responds to different biorhythms, as do hormonal secretions, energy levels, and the like, but I wouldn't doubt that it does. Maybe your particular rhythms are better suited to sex at unusual times of the day. Who says you have to be ready to swing every night?

Millions of men think there is something wrong with them because they don't get hard on demand. The myth has it that if a woman wants you, a real man will be raring to go, any time of the day or night. That is nonsense. Men have their preferences and their biological differences. There is simply no set time you're "supposed" to get aroused. I can't count the number of men who tell me they feel sexiest in the morning or the middle of the day or whatever. The only problem with that is it might be inconvenient. But in many cases the inconvenience is minor. They're just too inhibited to break their habits, or they're afraid their partners will think they're crazy. So what if she does? Convince her you're crazy like a fox.

Morning sex is an especially good way to break the routine. What a terrific way to start the day! So what if you have to skip jogging, or rush your breakfast, or get to work a little late? Morning sex can be as invigorating as a cool breeze. It's a wake-up call. It tingles the soul and tickles the fancy. In fact, a lot of men like it better in the morning because they wake up with a so-called "piss hard-on." A full bladder compresses the venous outflow from the pelvis, holding blood in the penis longer than usual. Hence the morning erection. Nighttime sex might be a better release of tension, but morning sex is better than a hearty breakfast. I guarantee that when you shower after a morning romp you'll like what you see in the mirror, and that will set the right tone for a good day's work.

Then there is the question of different sex practices. When was the last time you tried something other than the missionary position? Have you tried letting your partner get on top and control the action? Have you tried the doggy position, entering from the rear? How about not having intercourse at all but bringing yourselves to a climax strictly with oral sex or mutual masturbation? Any change might add a fresh dimension to your routine.

Along these lines, however, I must add an important caveat: *draw the line at unprotected anal intercourse.* In fact, this practice is highly risky even with the use of a condom. I have been surprised at how many heterosexual couples experiment with anal intercourse and how many enjoy it. Some are simply looking for new thrills. Others, interestingly, are looking for an alternative to vaginal intercourse due to religious or cultural reasons. In my practice I have seen an increasing number of women from Muslim cultures, where their religion prohibits sex before marriage. In their society, the sheets on the marital bed are examined by the groom's family the next morning, and if no bloodstains are found, severe consequences ensue. This prohibition has led many educated, Westernized women who have lost their virginity to request that I repair their hymenal membranes surgically before their wedding day so that the mandatory bloodstains show up on their sheets. Others have retained their virginity but satisfy the sexual longing of their boyfriends by indulging in anal intercourse.

This has all come to my attention in the last few years because people who practice anal sex, or are tempted to, have become concerned about AIDS. As a doctor, I must confirm that their concern is justified. It is no longer safe to think of anal intercourse as an occasional treat. AIDS is the bubonic plague of the twentieth century, and all the studies so far indicate that a primary mode of transmission is through anal sex. We believe this is because the anus is particularly vulnerable to tears in the tissue membrane. So until we know otherwise, unprotected anal sex should be off limits on the basis of the AIDS risk alone. In addition, couples indulging in the practice should be aware that there are other health risks as well. If the penis enters the rectum and is then inserted in the vagina it can contaminate the urinary tract with fecal matter, and that can cause a rip-roaring bladder infection in the female.

Oral sex is another story entirely. For men who have been deprived of the pleasure, it is an excellent antidote for boredom-induced penis weakness. The act itself has made many a reluctant penis as hard as a diamond. Remember, the mouth's sucking action literally creates a vacuum effect. This transmits a negative filling pressure on the blood vessels within the penile shaft, drawing blood into its channels. Psychologically, oral sex can add an element of excitement to a relationship. What a thrill to a man when a woman does something so loving and gracious. Many an older patient has told me that the sucking action of oral sex is the *only* way he can obtain an erection firm enough to penetrate.

And yet many women withhold this excellent form of stimulation because they have a negative attitude toward it. For one thing, they feel it puts them in a subservient position, perhaps down on their knees. Some women find it physically unpleasant if the man's penis touches the pharynx in the back of the mouth, touching off the gag reflex. Finally, women complain that oral sex is a one-way street, that they are giving a man pleasure and not receiving any. To which I say: First, there are many ways to position your body for oral sex; you don't have to be on your knees. Two, if you ask your man to refrain from thrusting because it makes you gag, his cooperation and a little practice should solve that problem. And third, all good sexual relationships entail giving and receiving; there is no harm in asking for something special in return.

I should note, however, that most women I meet in the context of my practice *enjoy* oral sex. They find the act erotic in and of itself, and many say it gives them a certain measure of control that the usual foreplay does not. Indeed, many women take great pride in their ability to use their mouths and tongues creatively. "I love oral sex," one of them told me, "because I'm damn good at it, and because anything that gives him pleasure pleasures me."

If your partner is reluctant to perform oral sex, explain to her the physiology of why it gets a rise out of a penis. Allow her to express the reasons for her reservations and try to assure her that there is nothing dangerous, dirty, or sinful about it. If she has had bad experiences with it in the past, assure her that you care for her too much to hurt her in any way. At the same time, let her know that it would mean a lot to you personally and that it just might add a whole new dimension to your sex lives.

A TIME AND PLACE FOR EVERYTHING

Gary was a young engineer who married his college sweetheart right after graduation. Soon they had a child. The marriage was going well in every respect, but things changed when the company Gary worked for was hit by the recession and laid off a number of engineers, including Gary. When he told me he was having penis problems, I assumed it was because his self-esteem had taken a big blow thanks to the layoff. This is extremely common. Next to sexual issues, the areas that affect a man's self-image the most are those having to do with work and money. When a man suffers a financial setback or comes up short in his career goals, his masculinity takes a beating and this can manifest in penis failure. It's as if the mind said, "You messed up, you're less than a man, so you must also be inadequate sexually."

I call your attention to this link between penis power and success in masculine endeavors, like work and sports, because it is very real and very powerful. In Gary's case however, it was not the whole problem. He had enough insight to realize that the layoff was an unfortunate turn of events that had no bearing on his masculinity. At first, his sex life was not diminished. But when his job hunting turned up nothing and the financial pressure mounted, he was forced to move his family into his parents' home. It was a temporary remedy, while Gary explored job prospects in other parts of the country. But it was during that period that he found his penis power dropping like the profits of his former company.

The reason? He was living in the house he grew up in, sleeping in the bedroom he slept in for eighteen years, with his parents just a few yards away. This was the bedroom he self-consciously masturbated in, hoping his parents wouldn't barge in. This was where he sneaked dates and nervously tried to have sex before his parents got home. Next to his bed was the end table in which he once hid his *Playboy* collection. The associations were too strong. Just being there triggered all the sexual anxieties of his adolescence. He worried that his parents might overhear him and his wife making love. He worried that someone might walk in. Much of this was subconscious, of course, but it was perfectly obvious to his penis.

When I suggested that the house might be the problem, Gary tested the hypothesis by checking into a motel with his wife. They had a sizzling weekend. Now he was able to laugh at the whole episode, and he quickly made other living arrangements.

Gary's situation is unusual, of course, but it is a good illustration of the relationship between *environment* and penis power. Location might not be as important in sex as it is in real estate, but it *can* play a major role. Noise, the wrong temperature, the possibility of being interrupted, negative associations— all these things and more can affect your penis performance. True, a superpotent man will rise to the challenge regardless of his environment. But everyone has preferences, and they really do make a difference. Some men like hard-driving rock 'n' roll, some prefer violins, others the cool sound of mellow jazz. Some like the room totally dark, some like candlelight, others turn the lights on so they can see their naked partner. Some are inhibited by the proximity of other people, some find the danger of discovery a turn-on. Some like a cool room, others like it steamy.

What are your penis's preferences? Does it perform better under certain conditions? Why not arrange your trysts to suit those predilections, or at least avoid situations that diminish your penis power?

THE SWEET SMELL OF SUCCESS

My patient Carl was a twenty-five-year-old actor with an enviable history of superpotent adventures. Then he fell madly in love. The sex was fantastic and so was the romance and the emotional connection. After a whirlwind few weeks, the couple decided to move in together. Shortly thereafter Carl started having erection failures. I thought for sure I knew what the problem was. I had seen it happen before. "Carl," I said, "you're getting scared. Living with someone for the first time is terrifying. You feel trapped, my boy. You're afraid of losing your freedom and it's expressing itself through your penis."

Carl wasn't so sure about that. He said he was happy to be living with someone. He wanted to continue doing so. He felt he was *more* free because he had someone he loved to come home to. So I probed. Had anything changed since she moved in? What was different? They hadn't had a fight. She hadn't started issuing demands or ultimatums. She wasn't trying to change him. She hadn't stopped wanting sex. None of the usual suspects. Then he mentioned something that hit home. She smelled bad. The odor from her vagina had become very unpleasant to him. When they were dating, his girlfriend was very conscientious about her hygiene. But living together meant she didn't always have the time or the motivation to douche and otherwise tend to herself.

Carl had not considered this a possible cause of his problem. A macho sort of guy, he thought that nothing, let alone something so seemingly trivial, should interfere with his penis power. Like many men, he blamed himself. But, in fact, he found his girlfriend's odor was so distasteful to him that no matter how aroused he was, as soon as she removed her panties he quickly became *unaroused*. He hadn't had the heart to say anything.

I have examined thousands of women in my practice and have adopted the attitude of an environmental engineer when it comes to matters of hygiene. The vagina presents a number of unique problems. Anatomically, it is a deep cavity with a relatively small opening and a large potential for expandable space within. It houses a variety of natural secretions, it gets very little ventilation, and hardly any light. This makes it a breeding ground for bacteria. Most women take pains to bathe or douche regularly, especially when they anticipate having sex. But it takes some modest effort for a woman to keep her vagina clean and pleasant-smelling. Plus, they don't always realize the effect that a strong smell can have on a man.

As I told Carl, difficult as it might be, it is important to *communicate* exactly what you feel about the situation and to gently persuade the woman to be more attentive. With two adults in a good relationship there is no reason not to suggest that she wash or douche or use a bidet before you get intimate. Odors and discharges might not be a romantic topic of conversation, but if it's the second most unpleasant aspect of sex, as a recent survey revealed, then it deserves to be discussed openly.

THE MOST UNPLEASANT ASPECT OF SEX

I know what you're thinking: if odor is in second place, what is in first? Well, about 60 percent of the men answered, "an unresponsive woman."

It has been my observation that what makes a penis the hardest is an *enthusiastic lover* in a conducive environment. I don't know if it is the psychological lift a man gets from knowing that he is capable of turning on a desirable woman, or whether it's some subtle physiological response to the odor of vaginal lubrication—whatever the reason, the penis definitely responds to a warm, moist vagina like one of Pavlov's dogs did to the bell. Therefore, the opposite must also be true: with a disinterested woman with a cold body and a dry vagina it takes an awfully strong penis to prevail.

From my experience, too many men take it personally when a woman fails to respond. They assume it's their fault. They think there must be something wrong with them. Worse, when *they* don't respond to the unresponsive woman, they panic. They think their penis has failed them. Don't pile all that onto your shoulders. Responsibility only extends so far. If you find yourself with an unresponsive partner, do your absolute best to excite her. As a superpotent man, be persistent and diligent. Learn everything you can about women's sexuality in general and about your partner specifically. What does she like? What turns her on? If necessary, make an effort to expand your repertoire and learn new tricks. In short, use every weapon in your sexual arsenal and make the most of a difficult situation.

However, if you have tried your best and your woman is *still* unresponsive, you must not let it affect your sexual self-esteem. You are not a failure if you have given it your best effort. Absolve yourself and move on. Your woman might have a serious hang-up, which is not your responsibility to fix. Or it might simply be a case of sexual incompatibility. It happens. There are matches made in hell, even for men of great penis power. Unfortunately, such incompatibility sometimes develops *after* a couple have been together and have been having satisfying sex. If that happens and you want the relationship to continue, by all means avail yourselves of whatever counseling or therapy is appropriate. But do something!

It pains me to say that many of my patients are stuck with partners who do nothing to satisfy a man's desires, and the men feel there is nothing they can do about it. They shrug their shoulders and blame themselves, and sometimes they run to their urologist for help. They don't need a urologist, they need to either remedy the situation or move on before their penises die a premature death.

INTIMATE INTIMIDATION

The joke goes like this: There are two gates into heaven. Above one gate is a sign that reads, "Men Who Are Intimidated by Women." An endless line of men stretches out from this gate. Above the other gate is this sign: "Men Who Are *Not* Intimidated by Women." There is one guy in line.

Intrigued, Saint Peter walks up to this lone fellow and says, "Tell me, my son, what qualifies you to be in this line?"

The man replies, "My wife told me to stand here."

Why does this joke get laughs? Because every man, even

the strongest, most self-assured, most independent, superpotent man, at some time or another has felt intimidated by a woman. That's one of the deep secrets men carry around with them. The strong ones laugh about it, the weak ones deny it. One thing is undeniable, however: a relentlessly intimidating woman is anathema to penis power.

What do I mean by intimidating? Let me put it this way. Most men like sexually aggressive women who let them know what they want and are up front about their desires. But every man has his own line that separates the kind of aggressiveness that arouses him from the negative kind that makes him want to run away. When aggressiveness is perceived as demanding or threatening, it can cause penis problems. The gestures, words, and body language of some women don't communicate "I want you," but rather "Put up or shut up" or "I dare you to satisfy me."

Why are many men intimidated by demanding women? Because such women put pressure on them to *perform*. If the demand is overtly challenging, it's like having someone command, "Get hard now!" That's tough, especially if what she's really saying is, "I'm checking you out. I don't think you're man enough for me. And if you're not, I'm going to let you know about it." Even if you have no previous history of penis weakness, a new, overly aggressive set of demands can trigger the self-doubt that lurks deep within the psyche of almost every man. Will I satisfy her? Will I measure up? What if I don't? And you know what happens once you start thinking those thoughts.

Never let yourself be intimidated. If you are with someone who has unrealistic expectations or puts too much pressure on you to perform, then reason with her. Tell her how it makes you feel. And if communication doesn't change her attitude, then consider the possibility that she's not a suitable partner for you. An intimidating woman is not sexy, she's emasculating. Don't be fooled into thinking that a "real man" would meet her demands without blinking, or that failing to do so is a sign of personal inadequacy.

While we're on the subject of intimidation, we should note that many a loving, good-hearted woman can intimidate a man without realizing it. One of the most common ways this can happen is exemplified by a patient of mine. He had been with his new girlfriend for six months and everything was going along fine. Then one night they ran into her ex-boyfriend. He looked like a movie star with the body of an all-pro halfback. Later the girlfriend told him about the other guy. She said he was the best sex she had ever had. "He was unbelievable," she recalled. "He could go all night."

Her intention was innocent enough. She thought she was sharing an important part of her past with him; the moral of her story turned out to be that the ex-boyfriend was a jerk whose abusiveness was obscured by his sexual prowess. It had been an important lesson for her. But her innocent attempt to share an intimacy with her new boyfriend had a chilling effect on his penis power. He started wondering how his sexual performance compared to the ex-lover, and he grew fearful that he would lose his girlfriend because he couldn't match the other guy's standards. The result was an outbreak of penis weakness. After going over the situation with me one afternoon in my office, everything came out. Naturally, his fear was all in his head. The girlfriend adored him. She was not comparing him sexually to the other man (at least she was smart enough to *say* she wasn't).

The bottom line is, whether it's real or imaginary, deliberate or unintentional, never *compare* your performance to another man's. All you can do is give it your best shot. If you do that, you should feel good about yourself. You are what you are. Your penis is what it is. You only have to be as good as yourself. Don't let yourself think about who your lover might have been with in the past. It doesn't matter if there are, or were, other men out there who can outperform you. If I were to compare myself to Jack Nicklaus when I play golf I'd never tee off again.

WHEN THE PROBLEM IS IN YOUR HEART

"I want you to check my testosterone level," my patient demanded. Marty was a forty-seven-year-old business agent who was in terrific shape and had acquired a reputation as a superpotent bachelor before he finally married Marilyn two years earlier. "I don't feel like making love to my wife lately, and when I do it I'm...well, I'm not the man I used to be."

I told him I would do a blood test just to satisfy him, but that I was virtually certain there was nothing wrong physically. That would normally be my hypothesis in such a situation, but in this case I happened to have good evidence. The patient and I belonged to the same club, and the previous weekend I had seen him and his wife arguing heatedly in the parking lot. I asked him how things were between them. His answer was circumspect, but I could tell from his body language that he was holding in a big bundle of anger.

"Go talk to Marilyn," I told him. "Straighten things out and your penis will straighten out too." I charged him an extra thirty-five cents for the psychiatric consultation and sent him on his way. His serum testosterone, of course, was normal.

From my clinical experience, I long ago concluded that the greatest aphrodisiac ever invented is love. And the opposite is also true: the biggest enemy of sexual desire is hate. For men in intimate relationships, nothing will make a penis slink away and hide as quickly as anger, hostility, or resentment toward their partners. And if they fail to express their feelings and resolve their conflicts, it gets worse and worse. Then, when they go through the motions of making love, their penises say "I'm not getting hard for her! Not after what you've been thinking about her!"

Indeed, my experience tells me that diminished desire caused by anger will lead to penis weakness as well. Of all the extenuating circumstances that can affect a man's sexuality the single most powerful is the nature of his relationship. If you are harboring animosity toward your wife or girlfriend, if you are rehashing angry feelings in your head without expressing them, if resentment has been accumulating in your heart like granules of dust so that it obscures the love that brought you together, well, how can it not affect what happens when you get into bed? That is why a man who aspires to great penis power should learn to deal effectively with his feelings and not let them contaminate his relationships.

With long-term partners especially, it is the heart that rules the penis. As time goes by and the fires of passion diminish and the novelty becomes routine, it is the emotions that guide the course of sexuality more than anything else. It is beyond the scope of this book, and of my professional expertise, to advise you on all the complexities of male-female relationships and the nuances of subtle emotions. What I can do is tell you what I tell my patients: *remove all the anger and resentment from your relationship*. Keep the love and affection alive. Don't take your partner for granted. Don't let your appreciation wane. Don't let petty animosities overshadow the qualities that have kept you together.

Two mature people with a strong commitment have the best potential for mutually satisfying sex, but problems still come with the territory. Every relationship has conflicts—about sex, money, children, in-laws, and the thousand annoyances that pollute all relationships—and every conflict affects your penis. Work things out. Deal with the inevitable difficulties in a forthright, honest manner. If you can't do it on your own, then by all means find a counselor who can help you. Get your feelings out in the open. That doesn't mean just venting your emotions, it means communicating in an atmosphere of fairness and mutual respect, where each party listens as well as speaks.

In my experience, a man of penis power is not afraid of showing his vulnerability. If he's angry it's because he's been hurt or offended, and he knows it's best to express his hurt feelings rather than hold them in and explode at some inopportune moment. If your relationship is built on a solid foundation, your partner will respond with equally genuine feelings, and the love that you've buried beneath your anger has a good chance of rising to the surface. When that happens, your penis is likely to rise with it.

10
You're as Old as You Feel

I
s it not strange that desire should so many years outlive performance?" as Shakespeare eloquently and perceptively put it. It might seem strange to men whose penis power appears to diminish as they age, but it is certainly not strange to a urologist. Of all the circumstances that affect the functioning of a penis, the most predictable is the normal, inevitable process of aging.

Far and away the most frequent complaint I hear is a variation on this: "Something's wrong, Doctor. I'm not the man I used to be." What they usually mean is: they don't have the same level of sexual desire as they used to; it takes longer to get an erection; it takes longer to ejaculate; it takes longer to get aroused again after they make love; their erections aren't as firm; some of the above; all of the above. These are all predictable changes that occur as men get older. They happen at different times to different men, but they happen to just about everyone who lives long enough.

Problems arise with either of two reactions to the process of aging: one, because the patient doesn't realize that such changes are normal, he concludes that he has a medical or psychiatric problem; or, he *does* know these developments are typical and concludes that he's hopelessly over the hill. Either conclusion is erroneous and detrimental to a man's happiness and penis health.

A typical example of the first kind of man is a colleague of mine. A radiologist approaching his fiftieth birthday, he had always been a man of superpotency and excellent general fitness. Noticing that he was getting cramps in his legs while running, he saw an internist. It turned out to be claudication, which means that his leg muscles were not being supplied with sufficient oxygen because their blood supply was decreased by a blockage in the arteries to the legs. He had the condition treated, then came running to see me. Because he had been medically trained, he knew that if the blood flow in his legs had been impeded the same might also be true of his penis. This was the explanation he had been looking for, because he had been alarmed for some time by a decline in his penis power. His ego had prevented him from saying anything to me, but now that he was sure it was a medical problem, he opened up.

After a complete uro-vascular profile, I was able to say without reservation that the blood flow to his penis was as good as it was when he was thirty. When I asked him to be specific about his concerns, it turned out his penis power was still at a very high level. The problem was, when he compared himself to what he was like five or ten years earlier, he was clearly losing ground. I said, "Do you run as far as you did at twenty-five? Can you lift as much weight? Do as many push-ups? Dance till dawn? You don't expect yourself to do those things because you know what happens to our bodies as we age. That's why athletes retire in their thirties. So why do you expect the same sexual behavior at your age as you had when you were a young man?"

The other response to aging is typified by the many men who resign themselves to a sexless life. Often they are worn out, ailing, cynical about life in general, and prone to complaining. These are men who enter retirement and stop living. As with a slight loss of memory or hearing, they interpret changes in their sexuality as a sign of impending death. They put their penises out to pasture without even a gold watch and a ceremony. What a sad waste of penis power!

The key point to remember is this: as you age, you do not lose penis power and your penis performance does not become inferior. It simply changes. It becomes different. Unless you have a legitimate medical disorder that interferes with penis functioning, you can be as superpotent at eighty as you were at twenty. The key is to understand the changes that come about with aging, accept them gracefully, adjust your attitude, and make the most of what you have. It's all relative. And it's all in your head.

PENIS PASSAGES

From birth until puberty the penis is basically a conduit for urine. The mechanism of erection, however, is present even before birth; male children get erections, but they are involuntary and not associated with anything sexual. These childhood erections probably occur due to nerve stimulation caused by a full bladder or rubbing the penis with a towel after bathing.

Then comes puberty, when peculiar things start happening. The testicles have developed to the point where they produce enough circulating testosterone (the male androgen) to alter the size and appearance of certain body parts. Now the boy develops secondary sexual characteristics and the ability to ejaculate. Suddenly the penis is a wonderful novelty. Boys can't play with theirs enough. Now they can be stimulated just by looking at a sexy picture or a girl's legs. They realize they can masturbate, and inevitably they learn that it can be even nicer with a partner.

Typically, when a boy reaches his late teens, he becomes sexually obsessed. His level of desire, the ease with which he becomes aroused, and his capacity for frequent sex are astounding. Dominated by hormones, physically fit, and not yet burdened by adult responsibilities, he is a walking erection, capable of getting one at any time with little or no provocation, and capable of ejaculating five or six times a day! At no time does the penis rule the brain more than it does in adolescence. I am reminded of the time a professor of mine brought down the house with a cogent observation. Princeton was not yet coed, so the auditorium was filled with a few hundred male freshman in a philosophy survey course. The professor looked over the students and said, "All you guys out there have this piece of beef hanging between your legs. These days, your whole life is fixed on that piece of meat. It's all you think about, day and night. If there were a way to channel the mental energy focused on your collective dicks into a more productive intellectual plane, you would all go through college Phi Beta Kappa and summa cum laude and save a hell of a lot of energy in the process."

The penis problems that I treat in patients in their late teens and early twenties are typically those associated with hypersensitivity. Unsure of himself, worried about whether he is normal and whether he is as virile as his friends, a young man might lose his perpetual erection at precisely the wrong moment because of sheer nervousness. More typical is the problem of premature ejaculation. The adolescent penis is extremely sensitive, the volume of semen produced is higher than at any other stage of life, and the young man has not had enough experience to develop self-control. Hence, he might ejaculate before penetration or immediately thereafter. This can be embarrassing enough to make a boy shy away from sex. If only he knew how typical it was! The solution for most young men is simply to have more frequent ejaculations. (However, in this age of AIDS, I must add a cautionary note: frequent sex should not be regarded as synonymous with indiscriminate sex.) In the late teens and early twenties, recovery time can be as short as a few minutes. If you ejaculated prematurely the first time, the next time you will last longer simply because there is less fluid in your seminal vesicles and less physiological urgency to release it. It requires a higher level of stimulation over a longer amount of time to get through the excitatory phase to where the reflex of ejaculation occurs. I will have more to say about premature ejaculation later.

I have seen a surprisingly large number of men with penis

weakness in their early- to mid-twenties. These are young men who suddenly find themselves having erection problems. It almost never stems from anything physical, even though, medically speaking, the "peak" of sexuality might have been passed at age nineteen or twenty. My observation is that it has more to do with the *stage* of life they have now entered: out of school, no longer in a safe, predictable environment where their stature revolves around popularity issues, and no longer protected by their parents. Suddenly they are dealing with the harsher realities of life and making "grown-up" decisions. The big man on campus is now a little man in the office. The star student now has to pass tests that are not on paper and not multiple choice. The girls he picked up in classrooms and fraternity parties are now young women with mature needs and demands. He finds himself in a real relationship for the first time, with all the complexity and confusion that implies. Also, for the first time he is working hard and for long hours, so he feels rather exhausted by Friday. Pressures and strains impinge on him that he can't easily shunt aside.

All of which often amounts to a high *stress* load for someone without the skills, seasoning, or maturity to deal with it. He has not yet developed the ability to compartmentalize his life. Such pressures often cause a young man to question his masculine identity. The result of all this can be a serious case of self-doubt, leading to the penis consequences we have already described.

Then come other changes. These continue from the peak period of sexuality until your penis is laid to rest with your other organs. Interestingly enough, these changes will not be seen in the penis itself. It is one of the most remarkable aspects of the penis, and yet another paradox, that it undergoes virtually *no change in size or appearance* as you age. While other organs degenerate, while your skin wrinkles and your waistline expands, while your hair gets gray and your scalp shows through, your penis looks the same as it ever did. If I showed you an unaltered photograph of a twenty-year-old erect penis side by side with one eighty years old, you would not be able to tell the difference. The same is more or less true of two flaccid penises, although the trained eye of a urologist might discern a subtle difference. In the elderly penis there is some relaxation of the suspensory ligaments (located just under the pubic bone), which give the impression that the penis has lengthened. This is more illusory than real; the penis is not really longer, it is just hanging differently. Conversely, there is no *shrinkage* of the penis with age, as many men fear. The length and width of the erect penis is dictated by the size of the corpora cavernosa (the tubular structures that fill with blood in the erect state) and that does not change once a man reaches maturity.

What does change is how the penis behaves. The first thing men notice is that it takes them longer to get an erection. This might start in their twenties, and it might happen so gradually that it is not noticed until they approach middle age. Much depends on the kinds of relationships they have and the frequency of their sexual activity. But at some point men invariably discover that it takes more to get them hard. Once your hormones stop rampaging, fantasies are no longer enough; the mere sight of a sexy body might not do it, nor even heated foreplay. It might require a little more direct stimulation from your partner. Indeed, in my experience, as I mentioned, many older men can get an erection only from the vacuum effect of oral sex.

As you age, you might also notice that your erections are not always as rigid as a steel rod, like they were during your teen years. Sometimes they're sort of half hard or semirigid, until added stimulation brings them to full strength. This too is normal, but men often greet it with panic, recalling the days when they seemed to spend half their time concealing erections.

The same is true of the refractory period. It is a well-documented urologic fact that the amount of time it takes to recover after an ejaculation increases in proportion to a man's age. When a man reaches his fifties and sixties, the refractory period might be as long as twenty-four hours, even with direct stimulation. Men also notice that the act of ejaculating feels less and less explosive as they age; the semen leaks out rather than being forcefully expelled. Also, orgasms might feel less intense.

All of this is a normal part of the aging process. You should anticipate these changes and greet them without bitterness or alarm. So what if it takes a little longer to get erect? You and your partner can enjoy the extra foreplay required to get you ready. So what if you can't go at it a second or third time without a long rest? It does not signify a decline in your manhood. You can't do a lot of things the way you once did, and besides you probably don't desire sex as often as you used to anyway. Just focus your attention on getting the absolute most out of the intercourse you can handle. So what if your ejaculations are not as volcanic as they once were? You can still enjoy the pleasure of orgasm to the fullest.

And besides, there is another change that occurs with age, and this one should be viewed as a bonus: it takes longer to climax. As the old joke goes, "It takes all night to do what I used to do all night long." But this is not a problem, it's a gift, especially if you found it difficult to control your ejaculations in the past. Young men who are quick on the trigger find their sex lives far more satisfying when they reach the age where delaying orgasm is no longer a chore but a natural process. Your partner will get more pleasure because it is usually easier to bring a woman to orgasm with prolonged intercourse than with quick encounters. And the more satisfied your partner is, the more aroused *you* will be.

The bottom line is, sex doesn't get less enjoyable with age, or in any way inferior. It just becomes different. And it can be better than ever if you have the right attitude. Not only do you naturally acquire greater ejaculatory control; if you have been paying attention over the years you should also have learned a great deal about women in general and your partner in particular. You should have learned tricks for arousing and satisfying the person with whom you share your bed—and vice versa.

One thing you might have to do as you age, especially when you reach your sixties and seventies, is adjust your *style* of lovemaking. Your penis might look as young as ever, but the rest of you has aged. You might have more control over when you ejaculate, but your arms might not be strong enough to support you that long. The muscles of your back and legs might tire quickly. Your joints and ligaments might not be as flexible. All of which means you might have to rest or change positions more often. Or you might have to try different positions entirely. If you keep a positive attitude you'll find all of this a challenge, not a burden.

YOUNG AT HEART, YOUNG IN PENIS

Attitude is the key to penis longevity. My superpotent patients tell me that sex gives them as much joy at seventy as it did at twenty. Some say it's even better. Equal pleasure can be obtained from occasional prolonged intercourse with one orgasm as with frequent, rapid intercourse and multiple orgasms.

The sad thing is, many men give up their sex lives as soon as they start identifying themselves as "old"—especially once they retire. The idea that retirement equals nirvana is one of the most unfortunate myths ever perpetrated. I have observed in my practice that retirement can lead to inertia, boredom, and stagnation. Many of my older patients, even those who are well heeled, choose *not* to retire. They might cut back their hours and delegate a lot of responsibilities, but they keep active. These tend to be my healthiest, most superpotent patients. They live longer and the quality of their lives is better than those who stop challenging themselves. My advice as a urologist is, don't retire your penis unless you're forced to by circumstances beyond your control, such as serious illness.

Until recently, our society's image of aging totally excluded sex. It has been considered unseemly for older people to even *talk* about it, much less do it. I know elderly people who have to sneak around to have sex, just as they did when they were teenagers, because they know it will be frowned upon by their peers and especially their own children. Other older people stop having sex altogether because they bought the notion that they're *supposed* to give it up. They suppress their sexuality because it somehow seems inappropriate to express it.

I hope that the generation I now see entering their senior years changes all that. You deserve an active, healthy sex life as long as your body can handle it. It won't harm you unless you try to do things your muscles and joints are too weak to manage, or you overexert yourself to the point of exhaustion. Just don't expect yourself to do at fifty what you did at forty, or at sixty what you did at fifty, or at seventy what you did at sixty, and so on. Adjust your sexual activities as your body changes, just as you adjust other activities. Look upon the adjustment as a new challenge. Use your mind and imagination to make up in creativity what you now lack in physical strength.

In my medical experience, as long as you are able to breathe, move your extremities, maintain reasonable control over your bodily functions, remain alert enough to identify the day of the week and the date on the calendar, and sustain a positive mental outlook, you can continue to exercise your penis power indefinitely. You can help stay superpotent as you age by maintaining good overall health habits: exercise regularly, minimize your consumption of fat and cholesterol, control your weight, avoid smoking and excessive drinking, watch your blood pressure, and see your physician regularly. If you stay physically fit and mentally alert, you can remain sexually active as long as you have the urge.

Most important, *don't think old!* Your body may produce less testosterone; your blood vessels may have become partially obstructed, diminishing the blood flow to the penis; your muscles and joints may have deteriorated. But if your mind is still strong, your penis can be strong too. The key is not to lament what you have lost but to be grateful for what you still have and make the most of it. Age is not a deterrent to a superpotent man, it's a challenge and an opportunity. Think of yourself as a singer whose voice is not as powerful as it once was, but who more than makes up for it with phrasing, feeling, and subtlety.

Think of yourself as an athlete or dancer whose legs are no longer as strong as oaks, but who performs with added grace because of the wisdom that comes with experience. If you keep your enthusiasm, you can compensate for, or even forestall, bodily decay.

If you have penis power, you are young no matter what your age might be. The strenuous use of your penis will sharpen your mind, exalt your soul, and keep you feeling vigorous. In short, you don't stop having sex because you get old, *you get old because you stop having sex.*

In fact, in many ways, your later years should be golden years for sexuality. Think of it: you don't have to get up and go to the office in the morning; you don't have to worry as much about kids and bills; you have less daily stress and fewer pressures; you have more privacy; you have more time; you can afford the luxury of patience. This is an opportunity for a superpotent man to make the most of his penis power.

Sex is not only safe for older men, it is good for them. It helps keep you young. Your penis is there to serve you, from puberty to old age. Don't give up on your penis and it won't give up on you.

PENIS POSTERITY

One good reason to be optimistic about the longevity of your penis power is that medical science is capable of helping you even if aging reduces the capacity of your body. The single most common cause of erection failure with aging is arteriosclerosis, which can restrict the blood flow to the penis and keep it from getting firm enough to penetrate. If a patient with that condition is motivated, we have lots of treatments that can help him. I described these options in Chapter Seven: prosthetic implants, vacuum or suction devices, and self-injectable vasoactive drugs such as papaverine and prostaglandin E.

With respect to the use of prosthetic devices and injectables, I want to make an important distinction between the type of patient for whom I recommend them and the type for whom I do not. A typical candidate is the man suffering from what I call Palm Springs Syndrome or Leisure World Syndrome. He is a widower in his late sixties or seventies, and he is starting to meet elderly women who like to go on dates. To his surprise, these women expect a level of sexual activity that he did not anticipate and is not necessarily able to handle. Typically, he hadn't been very active sexually in his latter years of marriage, either because of his wife's illness, his own reduced capacity due to impaired blood flow, or simply the diminished desire that accompanies long marriages. Hence, for the first time in years, he is called upon to perform, he *wants* to satisfy his new companion, and he's embarrassed. He feels like he's less than a man. If such a patient is in otherwise good physical condition, I aggressively offer solutions and encourage him to take advantage of them. He is a legitimate candidate for a prosthesis or vasoactive injections.

The other type of patient is an aging man who has been married for many years to the same woman and still is. The couple has had a fulfilling life together and remain very much in love, even though their sex life has diminished over the years, perhaps to the point of total inactivity. When they do attempt to have sex, the man finds he is incapable of getting an erection. Then, in a burst of forgotten youth, he decides he wants to have his old sex life back again and comes to me for help. If I feel he is seeking treatment in the vain hope that it will restore his youthful vigor and virility, I do not encourage implants or injectables. In my experience, if the marriage has already adjusted to the absence of sex, the treatments are not advised. I have found that once the novelty wears off this type of patient usually discontinues using the devices. Many a wife has told me that her husband used the prosthesis or self-injection a few times and then stopped. However, each case has to be evaluated on an individual basis, preferably with the wife involved in the decision. Treatment has, in fact, done much good for many marriages of fifty years and longer.

Let me close this chapter on aging with a prediction.

Based on my experience and my understanding of current research, I am convinced that the future bodes well for the sex lives of people now entering their senior years, and even better for those now middle-aged. I base this prediction on the amazing progress that has been made in extending the capacities of other bodily functions. The upper limits of what the body can do have been continuously broadened. In sports, what were once considered insurmountable barriers—the four-minute mile, the seven-foot high jump, and so forth—are now accomplished routinely. Furthermore, the peak years of an athlete have been dramatically extended by conditioning procedures, nutritional knowledge, and medical breakthroughs. I see no reason why the years of active sexuality can't be similarly expanded, and with it the penis power of aging men.

I believe that in the next century, people will be sexually active into their nineties. For one thing, lifespans will continue to increase, thanks to medical advancements, healthier lifestyles, and new discoveries such as the so-called Methuselah genes, which promise to prolong life through drugs or genetic engineering. Not only that but I predict that the *quality* of life in old age will improve geometrically. The elderly are far more vital and far more dynamic than ever before. In addition, society's attitude toward sex and the elderly is becoming more permissive. It will no doubt become far more acceptable to be sexually active into old age. And that trend will probably accelerate as the generation that came of age during the sexual revolution approaches seniority. For men who are young now, the golden years will truly be a golden opportunity for the enjoyable, leisurely exercise of penis power.

11
Questions and Answers

Because the average person knows so little about the area I specialize in, I spend a great deal of time responding to questions from patients, friends, and sometimes strangers. In this chapter, I will address questions that I'm asked frequently but have not yet covered or covered fully in this book.

Q. Do women prefer certain kinds of penises to others?

A. In more than twenty years of urologic practice I have had hundreds of conversations with women about the most intimate details of their lives. They have told me things they've related to no other person, including their most esoteric sexual practices and wildest fantasies. But no woman has ever seriously expressed a strong preference for one kind of penis over others. And believe me, I've asked. Length, width, appearance, complexion—these factors don't seem to matter, even to women who describe in great detail the kind of chests, legs, and behinds that excite them. When it comes to the penis, what they care about is *hardness* and *responsiveness*, although some also mention cleanliness. In a woman's eyes, the penis is a functional organ, not necessarily an aesthetic object. In that respect, women are no different from men; men talk about the shape and size of breasts, legs, and behinds, but you seldom hear them describe their preferences for vaginas, except to say that they like them moist.

Q. If I have sex a lot, can I damage my penis?

A. The chances of injuring your penis are minuscule no matter how vigorously you exercise it. Nature has designed your penis to be tough, resilient, and durable. It can take much more of a thrashing than most other appendages. Try twisting your ear or bending a finger the way you can twist and bend your penis. It can even withstand getting whacked around more than most organs, although I suggest that you take my word on that and not experiment on your own.

With the exception of whales, no mammals have bones in their penises. Therefore, there is nothing to fracture. Nor are there ligaments, joints, or muscles to strain or tear. The corpora cavernosa are surrounded by a fibrous tissue so tough that I have to work hard to incise it when doing surgery. When the penis is erect and these corpora are filled with blood, it is possible for severe trauma to rupture the fibrous sheath, but such incidents are extremely rare (this is sometimes called a "fractured penis," although it is a misnomer). It is also possible to rupture the surface capillaries of the penis, causing discoloration and bruising, but that too is rare, especially in the context of sex.

Just look at your own experience: how many men have you known who have injured their penises compared to those who have damaged their hands, arms, feet, or legs? If you recall any man complaining of a penis injury, chances are it had to do with the *skin*. Believe it or not, the skin is the most vulnerable part of the penis. It can suffer abrasions, cuts, and bruises, but these occur more often from accidents like getting stuck in a zipper than through ordinary sexual activity. Probably the most frequent sex-related injury is skin irritation caused by excessive friction. That keeps more men from having sex than any other possible injury, which is why one of my colleagues believes that "Vaseline has saved more marriages than Dear Abby." It is also possible to bruise the glans by thrusting against a woman's pubic bone. But again, traumatic injuries are more often caused by something other than ordinary sex.

Unfortunately, most of the penis injuries I see in my office and in the emergency room are self-inflicted. You would not believe the objects I have removed—not just rings and clips that perforate the skin, but long, thin items inserted into the urethra: pencils, pens, pins, wires, and especially swizzle sticks.

Bottom line: use it, don't abuse it.

Q. If I use my penis a lot will it get weak or run out of steam as I get older?

A. There is no predetermined number of orgasms, no quota, no upper limit that can't be exceeded. Nor will your seminal vesicles dry up if you ejaculate too much. Nature has not rationed sexuality. Sure, you get tired from having a lot of sex, the same as you do from *any* physical activity, but your body is smart; if you get too fatigued you lose your sexual desire. Get some rest and it returns promptly. If you use your penis frequently and vigorously it will invigorate the rest of your body and keep your spirit young and vibrant. Underuse is a much bigger problem than overuse.

Q. I have a history of heart disease. Do I have to limit my sexuality?

A. This is something to discuss with your cardiologist. Every heart patient should be advised according to his specific condition. However, I must dispel the myth that having sex is damaging to the heart. In the past, men who survived heart attacks were often told not to have sex. They were also told not to exercise and to retire from physically demanding work. All of this has changed. We now know that, within appropriate limits, exercise is good for heart patients. In that respect, sex is no different. It is not only a terrific form of exercise, it is unsurpassed in lifting the spirit of a man who has suffered the trauma of heart disease. In my experience, men with cardiac disorders often get depressed. They feel old. Their body image suffers. These psychological factors can impede their penis power, and there is no better antidote for such masculine malaise than having sex.

Having said that, I must issue an important caveat. If you have a history of heart disease, you should not be overdoing *anything*, including sex. As with any form of exercise, if you get chest pain when having sex, stop immediately and see your cardiologist as soon as possible. One problem I have seen frequently is older men who have both cardiovascular problems and retarded ejaculation. Because it takes them longer to reach climax, these men get caught up in a frenzy of exertion aiming for the elusive orgasm. This is like pushing the limits of your endurance to reach the finish line ahead of your opponent. It's fine for a well-conditioned man, but to someone with cardiovascular disease it can be extremely dangerous.

In conclusion, don't be namby-pamby, but don't try to be a hero either. Discuss your sex life with your cardiologist as candidly as you would your exercise routine.

Q. Is it possible to become addicted to sex?

A. From a strict medical point of view, the answer is no. Our criterion for addiction is the presence of physiological symptoms of withdrawal. When an addict is deprived of what he is addicted to he will suffer predictable biochemical consequences, as with alcohol, nicotine, or narcotics. Certainly, being deprived of sex doesn't feel good. Different men will suffer to a lesser or greater extent. But that does not constitute addiction any more than suffering over lack of food makes you a food addict or feeling restless because you haven't worked out makes you an exercise junkie. Like food and exercise, sex is a natural function.

It is perhaps more accurate to say that men can become compulsive about or obsessed by sex. In extreme cases this can be detrimental to other aspects of life. However, it must be noted that sexual obsession is not *caused* by too much sexual activity. It is not like taking cocaine or heroin; you don't become dependent or addicted by having frequent sex. Rather, destructive sexual obsession is a function of deep-rooted psychological problems. Men with that condition should seek the services of a qualified psychotherapist.

Q. If I take testosterone will I become a better lover?

A. Not unless your testosterone level is abnormally low to begin with. If it is within the normal range, injections of the hormone will not change your ability to get or keep an erection, nor will it improve your capacity in any way. In fact, it can be detrimental. Take enough testosterone and the chances are good you will end up in a urologist's office with changes such as shrinking testicles, just like athletes and muscle-builders who use anabolic steroids. What testosterone *might* do is increase your level of sexual desire, but it won't add a thing to your performance.

Q. My friends seem to be more interested in sex than I am. Is there something wrong with me?

A. There are vast differences in desire levels among men. One study of college students had the subjects press a counter every time they had a sexual thought or fantasy. Some students clicked in more than 300 times a day, while others reported that they rarely had a sexual thought. So who is to say what is normal and what is not? The important thing is that you are able to satisfy whatever level of sexual desire you have.

Q. I'm thinking of having a vasectomy. Will it affect my penis power?

A. Vasectomy is a safe, effective method of birth control for men who no longer wish to have children. The procedure consists of cutting and tying the vas deferens, the tube that carries sperm from the testicles, where it is made, to the seminal vesicles, where it is stored until ejaculation. Basically, vasectomy interrupts the passage of sperm, so that none of it is included in the semen you ejaculate. The procedure itself is performed in less than ten minutes in my office under local anesthetic through a nick in the scrotal skin. The postoperative discomfort is minimal and rarely requires pain medication.

As for penis power, there is absolutely no change after a vasectomy. There is no reduction in sensation, no lowering of desire, no less testosterone, no loss of ability to get or keep an erection, no less pleasure in having an orgasm. The only thing different after a vasectomy is that you release no sperm, but sperm comprises a minuscule portion of the seminal fluid to begin with.

Sometimes, in fact, a vasectomy will *increase* penis power because you are no longer inhibited by concerns about pregnancy. Longtime partners often feel more spontaneous because they don't have to interrupt lovemaking to deal with diaphragms or condoms, and they often feel heightened sensation during intercourse because there is no latex between the penis and vagina.

Some vasectomy patients change their minds about having children and request a reversal. Called vasovasostomy, this procedure involves reconnecting the vas deferens, a much more difficult procedure than the original surgery. It has, however, a high rate of success; most patients are able to conceive children afterward. And as with the vasectomy, the reversal does not diminish penis power. In fact, there is a potential bonus: because they are now making love with the express purpose of conceiving a child, the couple often find it more romantic than ever. Also, the typical vasovasostomy patient is reversing a vasectomy he obtained when he and his first wife decided not to have more children; now he is remarried, usually to a younger woman who wants to bear his offspring—a terrific turn-on for a middle-aged man.

Q. I heard that a "cock ring" will help me last longer before ejaculating. Should I get one?

A. No. In the hope of prolonging intercourse, some men place metallic rings around the base of their penises after an erection is achieved. Theoretically, the ring constricts the venous outflow so the blood trapped within the penis shaft can't escape and the penis stays erect longer. It sounds good in principle, but it can be dangerous. If blood flow is obstructed unnaturally—a definite risk with use of the ring—there is a danger of blood sludging or clotting, or rupture to the delicate sinusoids of the penis. The damage can be irreversible and make erections in the future more difficult to achieve.

I was once called to the emergency room at four in the morning. A man about twenty-four years old and high on some drug had a thick brass ring circling the base of his penis so tightly that it was eroding the skin. When examined, his arterial blood continued to flow into his penis, but the venous outflow was shut off and the penis was grotesquely engorged. He was in terrible pain. I told him we had to give him anesthesia and saw the ring off. I left the room to make preparations, and when I returned the patient was gone. He panicked at the thought of someone wielding a knife so close to his penis and ran from the hospital. I don't know what happened to him, but I do know that if you want to delay ejaculation you're better off with the squeeze technique described in Chapter Thirteen.

Q. Ever since my wife gave birth I don't feel like having sex. What's happened?

A. Sad to say, surveys indicate that this is common. One theory holds that postnatal changes in a woman's body might make her less attractive to her husband. For example, some women develop stretch marks on the lower abdomen or varicose veins in the legs, while others might find that their breasts have become less firm. Another suggests that the demands of parenting can make a mother haggard and exhaust a father. But in my mind, the main reason is this: after giving birth, the wife's attention shifts dramatically from her mate to her child. Now she is consumed by the child and the bulk of her affection and love are aimed at the baby.

For many women, giving birth brings a stronger sense of fulfillment than any other activity in their lives. It is normal and natural for her energy to be focused on her baby.

Unfortunately, even men who share that sense of parental satisfaction and appreciate their wives' commitment to the child might, on some unconscious level, feel rejected. Suddenly they are in second place.

Such postpartum changes are predictable. They require psychological adjustments, and possibly modifications in the timing and circumstances of your lovemaking as well. It is crucial that the superpotent man understand the dynamics at work and not interpret his wife's behavior as rejection.

Q. I want sex a lot more than my wife. What can I do about that?

A. In my experience, about a third of the couples seeking marital help do so because of a marked discrepancy between the desire levels of the partners. It's a common problem, reflected in the old joke: What do you call foreplay in a marriage? Answer: Begging.

No man likes to be rejected, even if he's secure in his partner's love and knows he's adored. And no man likes to beg for sex. But it's a fact of life: on the average, men have higher levels of desire than women and they find themselves in the mood for sex more often than women. Unfortunately, the problem can get worse if you suppress your sexual frustration. You run the risk of becoming hostile and resentful and letting those feelings out in ways that have nothing to do with the real issue. Or you might stop initiating sex altogether rather than face the possibility of rejection. You might even begin to shy away from all displays of affection. And, of course, you might be tempted to look elsewhere for sex.

In general, I believe that a superpotent man should do everything in his power to fulfill his sexual needs. Naturally, every man's ideal is to have his partner respond with enthusiasm each and every time he wants her. But in reality, coaxing, cajoling, and all forms of seduction might have to be employed, and even some subtle form of bribery (jewelers and florists can attest to that). No one should be reduced to actual begging, although I have a surprisingly large number of patients who are not above pleading. If it can be approached with a sense of humor, even that may be justified. Superpotent men are pragmatic: they do what it takes to get the job done.

But the best approach is honest communication. My advice is: break the silence barrier. Talk openly and honestly about your needs and the discrepancies in your desire levels. Educate your partner. She might not realize how frustrated you feel. She might not understand how demeaning it is to be told no. She might be perfectly willing to accommodate you, and to change her behavior so that you can express yourself sexually. But you must also be prepared to listen to her point of view, understand her needs, and negotiate an agreement that can make you both happy. You might have to make some changes yourself, like having sex at different times or initiating it in new ways. Whatever is required, if two people care enough to satisfy each other's needs, they can usually overcome differences in desire levels. If your efforts fail, then it's time to see a counselor.

Q. How come I seem to have more penis power in the summer?

A. When it comes to superpotency, hot is better than cold. That's why couples honeymoon in Hawaii, not the Klondike. It's not only the seductive ambience of tropical flowers, scented air, and hula dancers, but the physical effects of the climate. Have you noticed what happens to your scrotum when you plunge into a cold pool? The skin contracts drastically, the scrotal sac shrinks to the size of a peanut, and the testicles retract into the inguinal canal. Cold also causes vasoconstriction, a narrowing of the blood vessels. None of these conditions is conducive to penis power.

So why all the partying among ski bums and bunnies in frigid resorts? Because, after an invigorating day on the slopes, it feels downright tropical by the fireplace, or in the hot tub, or under a thick down comforter.

Q. My orgasms aren't as explosive as they used to be, and I don't release as much semen. Is there something wrong?

A. I get this question all the time. Invariably, the men asking it are in their forties (if they're older they've usually been carrying the question around for a while). As men age, their bodies produce less seminal fluid, so the volume of their ejaculate decreases. This is normal and natural. I assure you that the feeling of pleasure and satisfaction you get from an orgasm has nothing to do with the *volume* of your ejaculate.

Why do your orgasms feel less intense? Well, you still enjoy your favorite food, but eating it the hundredth time doesn't compare to the intensity of earlier meals. You still enjoy a good ball game or concert, but the thrill isn't quite the same as when you were a kid. But a more substantive reason for diminished intensity can be found in your mind. I have had men come in with big grins on their faces, saying that their orgasms are much more intense ever since they met their new lover. Believe me, the reflex of ejaculation hasn't changed. The difference is completely in their minds and hearts, where orgasms really take place.

Q. Is there any way to make my orgasms last longer?

A. This is one area where men are jealous of women. Call it Venus envy. For whatever reason, nature designed humans so that women can have prolonged wavelike orgasms while men's are brief and thunderous—five to seven seconds in duration. Wouldn't it be great, men dream, if we could make that ecstatic sensation last a full minute? Five minutes? An hour? Well, so far no one has come up with a way to do that. We have found ways to *delay* orgasm, but not to prolong it. (I am told that the Indian tradition of Tantric Yoga contains esoteric techniques for extending sexual ecstasy, but I cannot vouch for this.)

I will go out on a limb and predict that we will find a way to do it. With sex being studied by more scientists than ever before, I feel safe in predicting that researchers will eventually accomplish what individual men have been unable to on their own. When that day comes, it will be a great one for men.

Q. Do superpotent men masturbate?

A. There is nothing wrong with masturbation. It's normal. It should not elicit any form of shame or embarrassment. But I see it as a court of last resort for the superpotent man. Naturally, there are times when every man is alone, with no acceptable partner available. Under such circumstances, masturbation is certainly better than no sexual activity at all. In short, it will do in a pinch, but it is no substitute for the real thing. And given its negative connotations, too much masturbation can cause some men to doubt themselves; they can't help feeling a bit inadequate if they have to resort to mono when they'd rather perform in stereo.

Mutual masturbation is another matter entirely. Couples who know how to use their hands and fingers with the artistry of violinists can fill a bedroom with fantastically erotic music. So it's fine to let your fingers do the talking, but it's a whole lot better if the conversation is between two people.

Q. Does circumcision affect penis power?

A. There are no controlled experiments regarding the sexual performances of circumcised versus uncircumcised men. In my clinical judgment, however, there is no difference. Some people assume that the circumcised man has greater sensitivity because he has no foreskin covering the glans; other people think the *uncircumcised* man is more sensitive because he *has* a foreskin. Neither theory is true. The fact is that the foreskin retracts when you have an erection, so in the aroused state the penises are virtually the same.

Is it wise to circumcise the newborn? My opinion as a urologist is yes. Uncircumcised men have a vastly greater chance of getting penile cancer; in fact, cancer of the penis, which is rare in any case, is virtually unheard of among circumcised men. There is also the matter of cleanliness. If an uncircumcised man does not regularly retract his foreskin and wash underneath it, the natural secretions from the skin can produce a smelly, cheesy substance. Lack of cleanliness can lead to irritation, pain, and even infection. In addition, many women complain about the odor that results from failing to wash frequently and thoroughly under the foreskin. Generally speaking then, circumcision remains a healthier choice, but in all likelihood it has no effect on penis power. I do not recommend it in my adult uncircumcised patients unless there is a medical problem that warrants it, such as persistent irritation, infection, rash, or the inability to retract the foreskin for cleaning. Another legitimate reason might be that a man's sexual partner requests that he have a circumcision.

Q. My doctor says I must have surgery for prostate cancer, but I'm afraid I'll become impotent. Is there any alternative?

A. Let me tell you the story of a patient named Morton. He was a widower in his sixties who had recently married a forty-year-old woman with the perfect combination of beauty and brains: a former show girl who became a lawyer. Morton was having the time of his life with his new bride. It was as if he'd discovered the fountain of youth. Then we found a malignant tumor in his prostate. Given his age and the nature and extent of his cancer, the treatment with the greatest likelihood of cure was the surgical removal of his prostate. I recommended it and told Morton the truth, namely that we could be reasonably certain of curing his cancer, but, in spite of employing a nerve-sparing technique, we could not guarantee 100 percent that his ability to get satisfactory erections would be preserved. In short, it was a choice between risking the spread of cancer or risking his potency.

Morton was so terrified at the thought of losing his sex life that he insisted on an alternative treatment. Instead of the nerve-sparing radical prostatectomy, he opted for a less effective procedure because it guaranteed no loss of penis power. I literally pleaded with him to follow my advice. He declined.

Five years later, I learned that Morton was dying of cancer. The disease that had started in his prostate was now widely metastatic. Morton was a brilliant, successful man with a reputation for making smart decisions. But he literally sacrificed his life by thinking with his penis instead of his head and trading optimal cancer treatment for a transitory hard penis.

If you are faced with a decision like Morton's, pay attention to your urologist. He has vast clinical experience and years of training, enabling him to sort out all the variables. Have him explain exactly what your condition is and what the benefits and risks are with *each* alternative treatment. Get a second opinion, or even a third and fourth if necessary, but don't hold your life hostage to sex. If those vital nerves must be compromised in surgery to ensure complete ablation of the cancer, you can still be helped with a penile implant or injectable medication. As a surgeon, my first obligation is to cure your cancer. I will do my damndest to preserve your penis power, but not at the risk of shortening your life.

Q. What can I do to help my son grow up to be a superpotent man?

A. You are your son's primary penis role model. The smallest message from you—a nod, a grunt, a shrug, a casual remark—gets carved into his memory deeper and more indelibly than anything he picks up in a sex education class or a schoolyard. Set a good, responsible example with a superpotent attitude. A father who keeps his genitals under cover all the time, or never mentions the word penis, or avoids his son's questions about it will raise a self-conscious and probably self-doubting son. On the other hand, if you have penis pride, your son will pick it up by example, without your having to do much about it.

You can reinforce your good example by being candid and honest about penis matters without making too big a deal of it. Treat the penis as a fact of life, not as something dirty to be hidden behind a zipper or something of great mystery that can't be spoken about in public. Make sure you are his main source of information. Boys are extremely curious about their penises. If they suppress their curiosity because their parents evade the topic, they will come of age in ignorance or get their penis education the wrong way, from their peers. Don't pull punches or hide behind cute euphemisms. Be frank with your son, but be casual and lighthearted as well.

Let me give you an example. When my son turned nine, he asked me, "When will my penis be as big as yours?" I said, "Put your hand in mine. When your fingers are as big as mine, which they definitely will be, then your penis will be as big as my penis." Of course, I knew perfectly well that the penis is special (my son would not have bothered asking when his hands would be as big as mine), but I treated it as a simple fact of life, no different from fingers or toes. Naturally, the mere fact that a son can ask that question suggests that he grew up in an atmosphere of openness and had occasion to be naked with his father.

As your son grows, make sure he understands penis matters on a level commensurate with his age. Let him know you are there for him should he ever have penis questions. When they go through puberty and adolescence, *all* boys wonder if that organ is normal. Let him know that his penis is a jewel, a miraculous, pleasure-giving appendage that should be appreciated. Above all, find ways to reinforce his confidence in his penis. Let me give you a simple example from my own life. When I was a teenager, I was very self-conscious about being shorter than many girls at school. Once I came home from a party feeling awful. I told my father, "I'm real popular, I'm a good dancer, but half the girls are taller than me and I'm embarrassed to dance with them." My father responded with a big smile that let me know I was okay. Then he said, "You know, son, all girls are the same size lying down."

It was a simple man-to-man moment, but it had a big impact on me. In a subtle way, it instilled in me the confidence to approach *any* girl. (Later on, by the way, I learned that my father was right anatomically: there is relatively little size difference among people if you measure from the pubic bone to the neck; it is mainly the length of the legs that creates height differences. So when you're horizontal for sexual purposes height becomes irrelevant.)

One caveat: sexual candor does not entail prying into your

son's life. Teenagers need privacy. If you are *too* meddlesome and *too* up front, you can intimidate your son. You don't want to put pressure on him. Some fathers think they are instilling positive sexual attitudes by sharing sexy books or movies or alluding to their own exploits. Don't defeat your purpose by creating standards that make your son apprehensive and uncertain of himself. He should get the message that he and his penis are okay just the way they are.

Give him that message in every possible way. Superpotency is a matter of penis attitude, and penis attitude is a direct reflection of self-image. Do everything in your power to raise your son with healthy self-esteem. Let him know that he is loved unconditionally and appreciated for who he is, without regard to his performance in school or the playing field or with girls. Teach him to judge himself by his own standards, not yours or anyone else's.

Q. Can sexually transmitted diseases damage penis power?

A. Let's hold off for a minute on what should be your primary concern—AIDS—and talk about sexually transmitted diseases (STDs), which have faded from the spotlight but are still very much with us. In Los Angeles County alone, for example, one recent year saw a 57 percent increase in primary and secondary syphilis, a 108 percent increase in early latent syphilis, a 55 percent increase in penicillin-resistant gonorrhea, and a 149 percent increase in chancroid. The country as a whole continues to have a high incidence of genital herpes and chlamydia. The good news is, when diagnosed properly these diseases can be treated, and once the symptoms are gone they should have no deleterious effect on penis power. Let's describe the various STDs:

Syphilis usually begins with a simple sore on the penis. If diagnosed early and treated with appropriate antibiotics, the sores will usually disappear. However, if the initial diagnosis is missed, the infection can linger without symptoms, and it can develop into *secondary* syphilis, which is characterized by painful and highly contagious open sores. Eventually, untreated syphilis can infect the central nervous system, causing paralysis, insanity, blindness, or death. This rarely happens today.

Much more commonly seen in my office is gonorrhea, also known as the "clap." The patient usually comes in with a yellowish discharge from the penis. If not treated promptly, the infection can involve other areas in the urinary tract, including the urethra and prostate, causing troublesome scarring and strictures. Gonorrhea can usually be cured with oral or injectable antibiotics.

Even more commonly seen is genital herpes. As many as twenty million people in America alone are infected by the virus. It can lay dormant for long periods of time only to break out in blisterlike lesions on the penis, especially during periods of stress, exhaustion, or illness. Symptoms might also include fever, headache, burning while urinating, and discharge. When the blisters appear, the infection is highly contagious. However, to a healthy male (i.e., not immune-deficient) the herpes blisters are virtually harmless, although they can be uncomfortable. They can be treated with topical ointments or oral medication, and usually clear up completely in five to seven days. Herpes is *not* the scourge of the 1990s. It is a minor thorn in the side of a sexually active man, no more virulent than herpes on the lip, and people don't panic over that. Although herpes is *not* curable or even preventable, in almost all instances, it is no more than a transient, though often irritating annoyance—in healthy men and women whose immune systems are intact. The analogy is the so-called cold sore or blister on one's lip—perhaps unsightly for a day or two, but totally harmless. The same holds true for genital herpes in virtually all healthy men and women.

Chlamydia is one of the most common STDs in the country; some gynecologists say it is one of the leading causes of infertility in women. The organism is responsible for about 40 percent of all recurring vaginal infections that do not respond to traditional treatment and can cause nonspecific urethritis, an inflammation of the male urethra. Often there are no symptoms, but the infection can still be transmitted. If symptoms do develop, they are likely to include a watery discharge, swollen testicles, and itching and burning when you urinate. Once detected, chlamydia can be effectively treated with antibiotics.

I see some men with human papilloma virus, which causes warts that look like little cauliflowers on the genitals. The warts are not only unsightly (thereby inhibiting the expression of penis power), but the virus is highly contagious. The warts are removed with a topical medication, but stubborn growths might require electrocautering, liquid nitrogen freezing, or laser ablation.

With respect to penis power, genital infections can definitely cramp your style. Not only can they cause pain or irritation but no responsible man would engage in sex if it means infecting his partner. They might even cause temporary loss of libido and diminished capacity to obtain an erection. However, with proper medical care those problems are short-lived; virtually all common sexually transmitted infections, with the notable exception of AIDS, can be completely cured or are self-limited.

AIDS, of course, is a different story. The HIV virus that causes AIDS is found in bodily fluids and attacks the cells of the immune system, leaving the body so vulnerable to bacteria, viruses, and parasites that the outcome is invariably death. So far there is no known cure for AIDS.

While the two most susceptible groups remain homosexual men and intravenous drug users, the incidence among heterosexuals is rising. While heterosexuals face a greater statistical risk from drunken driving or not wearing seat belts, do not make the mistake of underestimating the danger. As Magic Johnson's dramatic announcement in 1991 demonstrated, this is not the time for uninhibited casual sex with strangers. Superpotent men who are not in long-term relationships have to adjust to a new reality. When you have sex with someone, you are, in a sense, sleeping with everyone she has been with for the last ten years.

As of this writing, the Centers for Disease Control in Atlanta recommend that heterosexuals protect themselves by having sexual relations only with low-risk partners. Unfortunately, it is becoming increasingly more difficult to delineate low-risk from high-risk partners, as the AIDS epidemic spreads at frightening speed. HIV positivity, once rare in the heterosexual community, now has a *rate* of penetrance in nonhomosexuals that nearly equals the spread among gays. Today the *rate* of new infection with HIV is highest among heterosexual teenagers (who have multiple sex partners) and lowest among gay white men.

The *rate* of new infections is also increasing dramatically among gay black men, in prison populations, and in those who have contact with contaminated needles, as well as in all heterosexual minority groups, particularly blacks and Hispanics. The lines of AIDS demarcation are increasingly difficult to define. For example, a woman, even though not an intravenous drug user herself, can nonetheless be infected with the HIV virus from a sexual partner who was. She can then, in turn, transmit the virus to her subsequent sexual partners, who in turn can pass it on to their partners and so on... less like the domino effect and more like a fissionable explosion. And that is exactly what is happening!

When picking a sexual partner, remember the template of his/her entire *prior* sexual experience is permanently tattooed upon you. Clearly those cultures or subcultures that encourage multiple sexual partners (the young men in the big city bath houses, or teenagers on a sexual rampage) greatly facilitate the spread of HIV. The anal-oral connection has classically been implicated as the primary route of spread (excluding contaminated needles and blood products) but fellatio by itself can also transmit HIV. The deadly virus, in fact, can find its way into your bloodstream through any minor break or crack either in your skin or in the mucous membranes lining any body cavity.

To be informed is to be armed in the war against AIDS. Since there is no cure, extreme caution in both your choice of sexual partner and your sexual menu becomes your only defense. When in doubt, either about a potential partner or a sexual practice, you must just say no. It is not enough to know that your partner has passed an AIDS test; the virus can be transmitted before it shows up in a test. In addition, you should heed the usual advice about using condoms and avoiding anal intercourse. I know condoms cramp your style (some patients compare it to taking a shower with their socks on). I know it feels a lot better without them. But your life is at stake. You can love sex even with latex. If you play by the new ground rules you can still exercise your penis power to your heart's content. You just have to do it with discernment, caution, and care.

Q. What can I do to prevent medical problems in my sexual organs?

A. Unfortunately, the genitals and related organs are sadly neglected by the average physician. Most physical exams don't even include a cursory examination of the area, perhaps because doctors find it embarrassing or distasteful to touch a man's genitals or examine the prostate through the rectum. In most cases they don't even ask questions about the patient's sex life, which could provide clues to physical disorders.

By far the most common urologic problem is enlargement of the prostate. For that reason, men over forty should insist on a digital prostate exam when they have their physicals. I know this can be uncomfortable and embarrassing, but it's a small price to pay for detecting the early-warning signs of trouble. In addition, if you experience any of the following symptoms, you should seek a urologic consultation:

- a weak or interrupted urinary stream.
- difficulty starting the stream.
- the need to urinate frequently, especially at night.
- blood in the urine.
- dribbling after you think you have completely emptied your bladder.
- painful or burning urination (dysuria).
- persistent pain in the lower back, pelvis, or lower abdomen.

Bear in mind that we now have many sophisticated, noninvasive tests for diagnosing prostate disease. For example, the transrectal ultrasonic probe which is only about as uncomfortable as a rectal thermometer, has revolutionized diagnosis. Using sound waves, like the sonar in a submarine, it enables us to determine the weight and volume of the prostate gland and view its internal structure. Pictures can be filed in the patient's record for comparison at the time of subsequent exams. And it alerts us to abnormalities that could be signs of prostate disease, including cancer.

There has also been another, even more important revolution in the early diagnosis of prostate cancer. Called the prostate specific antigen blood test, or PSA, this is to men what the pap smear and mammogram are to women: a routine, painless way to detect cancer in time to treat it effectively. The body produces a specific antigen in response to prostate cancer. The PSA tells us if the antigen is present at abnormal levels. If it is, we use ultrasound technology to locate the tumor focus, and then precisely biopsy the suspicious area, all in about one minute, without making any incision in the skin. I strongly recommend a PSA determination as part of a routine annual screening for men over fifty, although it's not a bad idea to start at forty.

New technology also enables us to detect various tumors in the urinary bladder or testicles, as well as any obstruction of the urinary flow. I should point out that the treatment of testicular cancer has improved vastly. Just ten years ago, 90 percent of patients suffering from certain types of testicular cancer were doomed to die within five years; now more than 95 percent are curable.

Unlike prostate cancer, testicular cancer occurs mainly in men under forty. Regardless of your age, however, I strongly suggest that you self-examine your testicles from time to time and feel for suspicious lumps. The best time for a self-examination is during a warm bath or shower, when the scrotum is relaxed. Your testicles should feel like hard-boiled eggs without the shells; smooth and void of lumps. Any lump, even a painless one, should be reported to your doctor instantly, whether you feel it during a self-examination or your sexual partner notices it while making love, as has happened with a large number of my patients. (Incidentally, if you notice that one of your testes is lower than the other, don't panic. One teste is *always* lower. It's nature's way to make sure those two sources of life don't collide with each other.)

With respect to prevention of prostate problems, I have one suggestion in addition to regular examinations: *have lots of sex*. Like all organs, the prostate benefits from exercise, and the best exercise it can get is ejaculation. When you ejaculate, perineal muscles contract violently. This provides a massage of sorts for the prostate gland, which should help keep its ducts open and fluids from becoming stagnant.

Finally, if you should ever experience a *sudden* onset of penis weakness, see your doctor immediately. Try to find one who understands that your sexual organs are not just machines that perform biological services, but are also psychological and spiritual agents designed to bring you pleasure. Make sure that your doctor is someone with whom you feel comfortable sharing the intimate details of your life.

Should you go to a sex therapist or psychiatrist? In my opinion you should first rule out all possible *physical* causes for your onset of penis weakness. If you do that and still want help, your urologist should be able to guide you to an appropriate professional.

12
A Word to the Wise: Women

The way to a man's heart may be through his stomach, but the way to his *soul* is through his penis.

That is the message I want to send out to all women. If I had my way, every woman would be a penis expert, a walking encyclopedia of penis knowledge, a wizard at enhancing penis power. My advice is: Help your man become superpotent. Learn everything you can about the penis—how it works, why it works, when it works, where it works. Find out what his penis needs, what it likes, what excites it, what makes it get up and go. Cater to his penis.

I say this without hesitation, knowing full well that some women will think it sounds retrograde or sexist. I assure you my message is neither. I'm all for equality—at home, at work, and in the bedroom. I'm all for women fulfilling themselves in every way possible. I am not suggesting that you become a sex slave, a bimbo, or a slut. I am not advocating that you become subservient or submit to any form of abuse or degradation. I am advising you to make your man's sexual satisfaction a high priority *for your own selfish reasons*. Make him happy and he'll make *you* happy. Give to him and you're more likely to get what you want *from* him. Quid pro quo. It's a simple fact of life, a basic principle of human interaction: we do things to please other people because we want them to treat us well.

And the Golden Rule is never more powerful than when applied to the penis. Do unto him and he will do unto you.

This works both ways, of course; I advise men to learn how to satisfy their women too. But women understand the principle better; they grasp it instinctively, I believe. Hundreds of women have taken me aside, whether in my office or at a party, and asked me what they can do to enhance their partner's penis power. They might not use those exact words, they might stammer and beat around the bush and conjure up every euphemism they can think of, but that's the message—not, I must add, because they're overcome by selfless generosity, but because they're interested in their own satisfaction. I have never met a woman who did not want a superpotent man.

IT BEGINS WITH COMMUNICATION

When I get a patient who complains about another doctor, the grievance is invariably, "He didn't communicate with me." I'm sure that marriage counselors and sex therapists hear the same thing all the time. It is impossible to overemphasize the importance of communication. If the man in your life does not let you know what he likes sexually, there are essentially three things you can do: forget about it, experiment, or ask. I do not recommend the first alternative; learning what turns him on and delivering it is the best way to improve his penis power. You can experiment, trying different things to see what works and what doesn't, but if your man is not the expressive type the answers might not be obvious. So experiment to your heart's content and add to the variety of your experience, but I strongly recommend that you also talk to him about his needs, desires, and fantasies. Let him know you care enough to ask. Let him know you want to satisfy him.

Some men are uncomfortable with candid sex talk. If that's the case, be patient. Get whatever information you can and wait for the next opportunity. You might also use a book or magazine article as a starting point: "I read that some men like . . ." And, of course, you can learn a lot while making love. There's nothing wrong with asking, "Do you like this?" or "Would you like me to . . . ?" or "Was that good?" He only has to grunt a response and you'll gather important information.

Naturally, communication runs two ways. You want to make sure *he* understands *your* likes and dislikes, because that information will increase his penis power. You can't expect him to read your mind, of course, so talk to him openly. But be sure to exercise all your diplomatic skills.

Men have extremely delicate egos, particularly when it pertains to their penises. If you want your man to improve his lovemaking abilities, use positive reinforcement as much as possible. Try to avoid saying anything that could be taken as a put-down, especially while making love. If you want to correct him or change his behavior, do it with delicacy and compassion, as you would with a child. Making him feel self-conscious will probably *diminish* his penis power when you're trying to increase it. Be honest and forthright, but focus on what you'd *like* him to do, not what he's doing wrong. If you don't like some of his techniques, instead of telling him so point-blank, try telling him what you'd *rather* he did. In other words, instead of saying, "I can't stand it when you do that to my breast," say, "I think I'd really like it if you did such and such."

Even delicate matters such as early ejaculation can be handled that way. Instead of saying, "I think you have a problem" or "Can't you learn to control yourself?" you might use words to this effect: "Making love to you is so wonderful. Wouldn't it be great if we could do it even longer? Let's try to work at it together." The difference is obvious. One form of expression suggests that he's inadequate, while the other says he's okay, you love him, and you want everything between you to be even better. Even if you think you're joking or innocently pointing out a problem, his fragile penis ego might take it as a put-down. If you say anything that makes him feel defensive, it will surely increase his self-doubt. And you know what that leads to.

Also, try not to come across as overly demanding. Nothing

is more intimidating to a man than a woman who makes unrealistic penis demands or issues ultimatums. If you say, or even imply, "Shape up or else!" a superpotent man might rise to the occasion. But more often than not, a man who gets that message will either never be heard from again or become so nervous that he has a penis power outage.

When your man does something you like, or if he shows any sign of trying to comply with your wishes, give him immediate positive reinforcement. Let him know you like it. Let him know he's on the right track. Let him know you appreciate the effort. Even if you have to exaggerate, get the message across. The slightest sign of pleasure from his woman will make any man feel a foot taller. It will reinforce his confidence, and that in turn will boost his penis power. You might think this amounts to treating a grown man like a child. Well, in a sense, it is. A man with an erection is more like a child than an adult. Besides, if it ends up making him a superpotent man, what's wrong with a little child psychology?

COMMON COMPLAINTS

In addition to the obvious problems—"He loses his erections at the worst times"; "He ejaculates prematurely"—both of which are discussed at great length elsewhere in the book, there are several complaints that I hear repeatedly from women. Here are the top ten.

1. "He wants to have sex when I'm not in the mood." Typically, men want sex more often than women, and many of them expect their women to deliver on demand. To a certain extent, I agree. Assuming her relationship is working on all other levels, a smart woman will do everything she can short of jeopardizing her health to enable her man to exercise his penis power. Naturally, there are times when it is appropriate to say no, and only a Neanderthal wouldn't understand that. By the same token, there are times when it is appropriate to say yes even if you'd rather be doing something else. In a good relationship compromise is crucial, on sex as well as other matters. If he's willing to give in on issues that concern you, why consider it sexist or exploitive if you give in sexually from time to time?

Every couple has to work out their own ground rules. But in general my feeling is, a woman who wants a happy, healthy man will try to be there for him whenever and wherever he wants her. The ultimate beneficiary of your generosity will be you.

2. "Sometimes he turns me down when I want him." In my experience, most men find a sexually aggressive woman a great turn-on. They love it when a woman initiates sex. They love being seduced. But it's also true that men can be threatened by an *overly* aggressive woman. So you have to find the right balance: let him know you want him, but don't come on so strong that he feels intimidated.

Of course, some men *hate* it when women initiate sex. The more conservative men feel that way for ideological reasons: they feel it is a man's place to get things rolling. Others simply interpret a woman's assertiveness as demanding. Try every weapon in your arsenal, and if he continues to be a reluctant lover it might be a sign of deeper problems in the relationship.

Of course, his hesitancy might be due to something unrelated to your seductiveness or your relationship. He might be too busy, for example, or stressed out from overwork. I often get this complaint from the wives of movers and shakers. My response is no man should be too busy to make love to his wife. I suggest doing what his business associates do when they want his attention: make an appointment. Tell him you want to set aside a definite time to devote entirely to lovemaking. Rent a hotel room near his office if you have to. What a great way to rekindle the romance!

3. "He's so businesslike when we make love!" It is commonly said that once a man with a hard penis reaches a certain point of arousal he loses not only his reason but his sense of humor, his vocal chords, and any semblance of refinement as well. The animal instincts take over. All that matters is ejacu-

lating in a warm hole. Gone is the playfulness, the passion of the ardent lover, the sweet words, the grace and the charm. Suddenly he's mute at the same time that he's wild and flailing.

Well, if you're looking for the elegance of Cary Grant or the smoothness of Fred Astaire, you might have to rethink your expectations. If you want a more playful man, one who can laugh and have fun when making love instead of taking it so seriously, you have a better chance of getting somewhere. Many men get overly serious because they're nervous about their performance. They're afraid that if they lighten up they'll lose their desire, or their erection. You might be able to lead the way to laughter by taking the initiative and making him feel as unpressured as possible. As for whispering in your ear and telling you he loves you, if you do it first and he can't return the sentiment, have a talk with him—*after* you make love. It's hard to teach passion, but a satisfied man might be willing to work on his manners.

On the whole, women often have to accept the fact that men *can* be all business when they're turned on. Sex is the ultimate in goal-oriented behavior. You have to assess for yourself which of your man's traits you have a chance of changing and which you'll have to learn to accept.

4. "Sometimes he does things that hurt me." Sex should provide mutual pleasure, not pain. I hear two kinds of complaints in this regard. The first has to do with clumsy or rough behavior during foreplay: he bites her nipples like they were cookies, he rams his fingers into her vagina like a battering pole, he rubs her clitoris like he's polishing his car. He might lose his head to lust and become insensitive to his partner's feelings. He might have acquired some crude, clumsy habits when he first started having sex and no one has ever smoothed out his rough spots. Or he might simply be ignorant. He might actually think you *like* what he's doing. He might have even known women who *did* like it. You absolutely must let him know he's hurting you. But if you can possibly help it, don't whine or get angry. Tell him gently so he doesn't take it as criticism or a sign of failure.

The other kind of pain that's reported occurs during intercourse: too much internal friction (which might be solved by a vaginal lubricant); thrusting too hard against her pubic bone; yanking or twisting her body in an awkward manner; leaning his weight on a tender spot. In such cases, you have to help him change his habits. One source of pain, however, is biologically determined: his penis is too big. As I've already mentioned, I have had many more requests to make a husband's penis shorter or thinner than to make it longer or wider. Unfortunately, there is no medical solution. The answer is to adjust the angle of penetration and the depth of insertion until you find a combination that is both satisfying and comfortable. Remember also: there is no rule that says a penis has to penetrate to its full length.

5. "He wants me to do things I find distasteful." Unless he's forcing you to do something dangerous or painful, you might want to ask yourself if you're being too prudish.

As I mentioned earlier, many women complain that their husbands expect them to perform oral sex, which they find abhorrent. If you are one of those women, you should not feel ashamed of your reluctance to take his penis in your mouth. On the other hand, you should examine the source of your resistance; there is nothing inherently dangerous, dirty, or evil about oral sex. Many women find it extremely stimulating, especially if they're madly in love with their partners and enjoy giving them pleasure.

Perhaps your problem is not so much having a penis in your mouth but the possibility of swallowing semen. If so, you might have to negotiate with your man. Offer to do it only until he is ready to ejaculate. While many men find it incredibly exciting to climax in their partner's mouth, you might be able to work out a compromise. However, you should also know that, medically speaking, there is no danger in swallowing semen unless, of course, it is infected. Semen is not a waste product like urine. Quite the contrary, it is the most vital fluid in the male body; without it, human life would be extinct. Nor does ingesting semen produce negative side effects. Some women do get nauseated by it, but in my experience this is more of a psychological reaction than a medical one. For the most part, it is simply a matter of taste. Perhaps one day medical science will find ways of altering the flavor of semen, making it more palatable to women who have an aversion to it.

6. "My husband is a wham-bam-thank-you-ma'am kind of guy. And all he knows is the missionary position." Educate him. In a gentle way, let him know that you enjoy being intimate with him so much you'd like to savor the experience by slowing down. What's his rush? An extra few minutes of loving fore-play or passionate intercourse will bring *both* of you heightened pleasure. At the same time, bear in mind that there are times when every man acts as if he is in a race to ejaculate. Some-times they are simply overcome by physical need and their instincts take over, even if their minds are screaming, "Slow down!" If such occurrences are the exception, not the rule, you should be able to tolerate it from time to time, even if it means that only one of you leaves the bed satisfied. But this does not mean you should tolerate crude or thoughtless behavior.

As for trying new things, if he has no imagination lend him yours. Make explicit suggestions. If that doesn't work, try nonverbal communication—take the bull by the horns and maneuver creatively until you make him an offer he can't refuse.

7. "My lover doesn't want me to touch his penis." This is not a common problem, but it is a sad one. For a woman who wants to express her affection by caressing the manhood of her loved one, it can be terribly unpleasant to have her hand pushed aside. It occurs most often in new relationships, and it usually stems from one of two things: the man is afraid of premature ejaculation and feels that direct stimulation will speed him up too much; or, he has an abnormal, deep-rooted fear of being touched. The first scenario is easier to deal with and usually improves as soon as the man feels secure in his performance; the second is more intractable and could take a lot of time and patience. I recommend gradual steps to make him comfortable with the idea of being touched. The longest journey begins with the first step. So instead of *grabbing* his penis, start by stroking it with one finger for a short amount of time, or rubbing it with your thigh or arm, and work your way gradually to normal manual stimulation. Treat his reluctant penis with kid gloves until his fears dissipate.

8. "Sometimes he annoys me so much I can't bring myself to have sex with him even though I'm horny." To be blunt, get over it. If there is a deep, serious rift in the relationship, by all means work it out, either privately or with a marriage counselor. But if you're talking about the normal run-of-the-mill irritations that afflict every relationship, don't let them get in the way of sex. If you do, not only will both of you end up frustrated, but you will be neglecting the best solution to your problem. Remember Sutton's Law: when the infamous bank robber Willie Sutton was asked why he robbed banks, he replied, "Because that's where the money is." Well, I say satisfy your man's penis because that's where his soul is. After a good roll in the hay, he will be much more amenable to listening to your grievances.

9. "When my husband has a few drinks all he wants to do is have sex, but I don't like him in that condition." If your man needs a little booze to lower his inhibitions or to free his mind of troubles, it's not a bad thing. Unfortunately, as many women have told me, too much alcohol can turn an amorous man into a clumsy, insensitive brute. It can also keep his penis from reaching the launching pad. Like other problems, this one requires communication. You have to tell him why you prefer to make love when he *hasn't* been drinking—and if you want to be understood, make sure you have the conversation when he's sober.

10. "I'm a single mother. How can I educate my son about penis power?" One thing you can do is provide your son with unconditional love and let him know at every possible opportunity that he's worthy of his own self-respect. If you raise a healthy, self-assured son, the chances are he will feel secure in his penis image. As to the details of a young man's penis education, you can provide him with facts as easily as a man

can, but you can't speak from experience and you can't be a role model. If you have a male relative or a close male friend who can take your son under his wing, you can compensate in some measure for the absence of a father. Indeed, if the surrogate is a man of true superpotency, his presence might serve your son's penis education better than a real father who is not.

PENIS-ORIENTED WOMEN HAVE MORE FUN

They not only have more fun, they have better marriages, more faithful husbands, happier homes, and greater personal fulfillment in all aspects of their lives. I assure you that if women spent as much time attending to a man's penis as they devote to their hair, makeup, and clothing, they would get more of what they want and have more-satisfying relationships. If you accept the premise that men are dominated in large measure by the imperatives of their penises, and if you believe that each partner has the responsibility to satisfy the other's needs, then it follows that you will hold up your end of the bargain best by making his penis one of your top priorities.

Being penis-oriented does not mean selling your soul to the devil. It does not make you less of a feminist or less than an equal to the men in your life. It does not require that you sacrifice your intelligence or your self-respect. It simply means learning to understand and accommodate a man's penis needs and approaching that task with all the pride and skill that you would bring to any other endeavor. I assure you, based on all my clinical experience, that you and your man will reap rewards you have only dreamed about.

13

How to Become a Superpotent Man

Every man can be superpotent. *You* can be superpotent. That is the bottom line, and this is the bottom line chapter. I am going to describe some practical steps you can take to maximize your penis power. But before I do I must emphasize one point: the most important steps you can take are to work hard to maintain physical fitness and cultivate a happy, upbeat attitude about life as a whole. Superpotency is nothing more than life energy expressed through your penis power. Happy, healthy men have happy, healthy sex lives, and vice versa.

More specifically, you should develop in yourself the qualities of a superpotent man. If you emulate these as closely as possible it will make all the other ways to increase penis power more effective.

EDUCATE YOURSELF

I want to reiterate how constantly amazed I am by men's ignorance of sex and women. I have known men with world-class minds, wide-ranging experience, and excellent educations, but who don't know the first thing about women's sexuality or that of their own partners. They don't know a clitoris from a cuticle. Not because they aren't interested in sex. On the contrary, they are *very* interested in sex and they complain that they can't figure women out, but they still don't take the trouble to educate themselves. From my experience, their attitude comes from being overly interested in their own satisfaction and not their partner's.

This is the wrong attitude for a superpotent man. You should care a great deal about satisfying your partner's needs and desires, not just for reasons of equality and generosity but for pure self-interest. I'm not sure about the rest of life, but in sex you really do reap what you sow. It really is better to give than receive, because nothing excites a penis more than a wildly responsive woman. Satisfy her and she will react by finding ways to pleasure you on a higher plane.

We all know that women are different from men, but it behooves a man of penis power to understand *exactly how*. This is not the place for a complete treatise on the subject; there are many books devoted entirely to women's sexuality. But I would like to single out one point that many men in my practice don't fully appreciate. For physiological reasons, women in general take longer than men to get aroused. As one of my patients observed, women are like radio tubes; it takes them time to warm up. Men are like transistors: solid-state and turned on instantly. For this reason, women often complain that men denigrate foreplay, and men complain that women want to fool around too much before getting down to business.

My opinion is, each partner must learn to accommodate the other. If sometimes a man is so turned on he has no time for the niceties of foreplay, a woman should understand. And a man should appreciate a woman's desire for the subtle sensual pleasures of foreplay and learn to satisfy this need with patience and generosity. If you are impatient with foreplay, you might be missing out on some of life's sweetest pleasures. You are also depriving yourself of the great satisfaction that comes from giving pleasure to your partner. In my experience, men who learn to satisfy a woman's needs prior to intercourse find that their penis power increases measurably.

Even more important than understanding women's sexuality in general is to learn about your partner. There is tremendous variation among women. They have a vast range of likes and dislikes. You should never assume that the woman you're with fits some stereotype or a description of the average. Honest one-to-one communication is vital. Many men are uncomfortable talking about sex with women, even one they've been with for years. But if you want to be a superpotent man, break the ice. Find out what pleases your woman most. Find out what she really desires, what she fantasizes about, what she wants you to do more of and less of. A woman who is open and honest is one of the best allies a penis can have.

Equally important is a woman who is responsive to *your* needs. It's amazing how many men complain that their wives don't do enough of this or do too much of that, when they never bother to discuss it with them. You should be up front about your preferences. Communicate in a loving way, with no pressure, criticism, or ultimatums. If she is willing to make the effort it will do wonders for your penis power. If she is *not* willing to make the effort, then you might be in a sexually incompatible relationship, or you might have to sort out some of the deeper reasons for her resistance. Unless your desires run to dangerous sex, you deserve to have them met, but you have to be willing to meet your partner halfway.

A final word about learning about sex: don't overdo it. If you overintellectualize you might create an impediment. You can get so bogged down with facts and diagrams and psychological theories that you end up being more self-conscious and inhibited than when you started out. You end up thinking too much and losing the spontaneity and passion that makes sex wonderful. If you overanalyze it, you paralyze it. Your penis will say, "Wake me when you stop thinking so much."

GOOD HEALTH EQUALS GOOD PENIS POWER

The general condition of your mind and body is reflected in your penis power. Hence it is vital for superpotent men to maintain a high level of well-being, mentally and physically. Here are some basic tips.

Get fit and stay fit. A good exercise program is central to sexual fitness. For one thing, it takes energy and strength to make love. The muscles of your arms, legs, back, and abdomen are all involved; if they get flabby, your penis risks becoming flabby as well. So build up your muscular strength with weights, push-ups, sit-ups, or whatever suits you. Not that you have to be muscular, just strong and flexible.

Even more important, work on your cardiovascular fitness. A vigorous half hour of aerobic exercise four or five times a week is desirable. Physical inactivity leads to deterioration of your body as a whole and your penis in particular. If you start wheezing and gasping for breath while making love, your penis will get the message that you need to rest, and that's exactly what it will do.

Also, pay attention to what you eat. A diet low in fat and high in fiber is most compatible with superpotency. We have discussed the importance of blood flow in getting and keeping an erection, so it's obvious that superpotency depends on clean arteries and veins. Don't gum up the works with saturated fats and cholesterol. And if you've ever made love when you felt bloated or constipated, you know how much better you function when your digestive system is not overtaxed. So don't overeat and make sure you get plenty of fiber. Wining and dining can be romantic, but the romance withers if you overdo either one: too much alcohol (or any intoxicant) might increase your desire but will surely diminish your penis power; too much dining and you'll feel sluggish, heavy, and tired.

Another advantage to a lifestyle punctuated by prudent exercise and wise eating habits is weight control. Let's face it, it's a lot easier to operate smoothly and vigorously in bed if you're not carting a twenty-pound belt of blubber around your waist. Also, to most women, a lean physique is a lot more attractive. But even more important is *your* perception of your body. If you are overweight, looking down at your penis from above a big belly, you might start thinking of it as small because so much of it is obscured by layers of fat. And that, in turn, will cause you to *think* small about your penis power.

In general, I have found that men with poor body images have some degree of penis weakness, whereas men who are comfortable with their bodies and are content with their looks score high in superpotency. And believe it or not, men with positive body images are not necessarily hunks. In fact, some good-looking, well-built men have far *worse* body images than guys with ordinary bodies. It's all in how you see yourself. Some men are so insecure and vain that if they don't see Mel Gibson when they look in the mirror they hate their bodies. Others are content with what nature gave them, as long as they stay in reasonable shape.

Don't hold your penis power hostage to the youth cult perpetrated by the media. Images of sleek, muscular bodies with gorgeous women at their sides promoting everything from deodorant to pickup trucks are detrimental to superpotency. Whose self-image could possibly live up to those standards? If you eat right, exercise, and maintain a sensible weight you'll feel good about your body. And if you feel good about your body, you'll feel good about the organ that embodies your penis power.

In addition, get plenty of rest. Superpotent men tend to live balanced lives. They are energetic, busy and productive, but they are not workaholics in the obsessive sense of the word. In my experience, many workaholics seem to be running away from something. If they drown themselves in work just to make up for some deep feeling of inadequacy, they often jeopardize good relationships with their girlfriends or wives. Superpotent men, on the other hand, are usually just as *productive* as workaholics, and they work just as hard, but they also work *smart;* they know when and how to relax, and their capacity for fun is as big as their capacity for work. They have that seemingly uncanny ability to compartmentalize their lives.

In addition to good physical health, penis power requires sound mental health. I have already discussed the need to reduce stress, tension, anxiety, depression, and other enemies of penis power. It bears repeating here; stress will weaken you physically, interfere with the biochemical action needed to produce erections, and possibly lower your self-image to the point where you doubt your manhood.

Numerous studies have shown that people who undergo major traumas, such as the loss of a loved one or an accident, are much more likely to experience a serious illness. I can add unequivocally that they are more likely to exhibit penis weakness as well. I have seen many patients suffering from post-traumatic syndrome, and I can tell you that their penises often behave just like the men themselves: confused, frightened, and helpless. But with my superpotent patients, traumas don't seem to have such a devastating impact. They appear to deal with crisis effectively, and when it's over they put it behind them and their stressful encounter fades quickly from their minds. If you don't learn to do likewise, traumas large and small will pollute all aspects of your life, especially your penis power.

PENIS POWER EXERCISES

One particular form of exercise is the best way to develop superpotency: having sex. Practice makes perfect in bed just as it does in a sports stadium or concert hall. The more you use your penis, the more control you have over its functioning, and the more you learn about using it. As was once said about voting in Chicago, do it early and do it often.

In addition, making love is a great form of exercise for your whole body. Vigorous sex will increase the volume of oxygen taken into your lungs, quicken your heart rate, and raise your effective circulating blood volume, all of which benefit your general health. Sex can also help you moderate potentially dangerous habits. When you are sexually satisfied you feel so good about yourself you are less likely to abuse drugs, alcohol, or junk food. Finally, sex is a great antidote for stress. If you're feeling anxious or worried, if you need to get your mind off things and work off some tension, think of your penis as a hero in a white hat coming to the rescue.

Just as there are specific exercises to help you improve in a sport, there are ways to improve your penis power by strengthening the muscles used during sex. There is no sense exercising the penis itself because it is, physically speaking, a passive organ. However, you *can* exercise other body parts that serve the penis in its role as leader of the sexual brigade. This will give you greater control of your movements, as well as added stamina, strength, and flexibility. You are also likely to notice an increase of confidence in your penis power.

One suggestion is to do push-ups or weight exercises that use the same basic motion—pushing and pulling with the upper arms and chest muscles. To the extent that you support your body with your arms while making love, this conditioning will help prevent fatigue, so your penis won't think, "Hurry up and get this over with." Squats, knee bends, or other exercises for the upper legs will also indirectly strengthen penis power, since those muscles help support you during various sexual acts.

Maybe Elvis Was On to Something

Even more important is to exercise the muscles of the pelvic area. For obvious reasons, if you have control of your pelvis, your penis will function more creatively and dynamically. To accomplish this, I strongly suggest working on the muscles of the abdomen and lower back. Sit-ups, crunches, leg raises, and similar exercises will help a great deal. More to the point, I advise working on the flexibility of the pelvic region itself.

This might sound odd, but one of the most potent exercises you can do is to whirl a Hula-Hoop. These toys that were so popular in the 1950s are still around, and if you can work out with one a few minutes a day you will find that you attain much greater mobility of your pelvis. This will increase your potential for superpotency by giving you more control of motion during intercourse. It will also improve the circulation to the organs in the pelvic area. In the absence of a Hula-Hoop, you might spend a few minutes a day wiggling and rotating your hips, and thrusting your pelvis in and out like a hula dancer. If you do this to music, it will be more fun, especially if you have ever fantasized being a male stripper. No kidding: it really works!

PELVIC CONTROL

A more systematic form of pelvic exercise was developed by a colleague of mine, Lucien Martin, a chiropractor in Santa Monica, California. Dr. Martin created a series of exercises to strengthen the muscles of the lower back and abdomen for patients with back problems. But to his surprise, his patients reported dramatic improvements in their sex lives. He developed the exercises further and continued to get the same reports. According to Dr. Martin, the exercises strengthen the muscles and ligaments of the pelvis, lower back, and abdomen, and seem to improve nerve sensitivity in that area. Here are Dr. Martin's instructions for his Pelvic Control Technique.

Lie on your back on the floor or a very firm bed, arms at your sides. Place a tightly rolled towel of three to four inches in diameter under your neck, not your head. Under your knees place a thick pillow so that your lower back rests flat on the floor. Now, without lifting your lower back off the floor, pull your pubic bone toward your chest. Don't suck your stomach in. The idea is to lift the pelvis by *squeezing* the abdominal muscles like an accordion, not to pull them inward.

Lock the pelvis in the compressed position for a second, then relax. Then repeat, again and again. To make sure you are doing it correctly, press your lower abdominal muscles with the fingers of both hands as you do the squeeze. You should feel those muscles contract. Another way to test yourself is to press the abdominal muscles while raising your head and legs slightly; you should feel the compression of the muscles used during the exercise.

Proper breathing is important. Keep your throat and mouth relaxed, and as you squeeze your abdominals let the motion of the pelvis expel the air from your lungs. Don't breathe out forcefully and don't hold your breath. Just exhale smoothly as you contract the abdominals and inhale as you relax.

The exercise should be brief and vigorous. Hold each contraction for about a second and continue the repetitions for two to three minutes. Once you gain good control you can set a goal of 100 repetitions per day. One note of caution: if you have acute lower back problems don't undertake this exercise without consulting your orthopedist.

THE HARDER THEY COME

Superpotency is not only about getting an erection at the right time. It also entails controlling the timing of your orgasm to provide maximum satisfaction for you and your partner. As I mentioned, problems with ejaculation come in two basic categories: too fast and too slow.

The latter, which we call retarded ejaculation, can be caused by medical factors such as spinal cord injury or diabetes, as well as by substance abuse or the side effects of certain medications. In rare instances, the problem is so extreme that a man may be unable to ejaculate at all. Obviously, this requires the attention of a urologist. In other cases, the problem is psychological in origin. Some men can masturbate to climax and have nocturnal emissions, but they cannot ejaculate in a vagina. Usually rooted in self-doubt, repressed traumas, fear of pregnancy, or anxiety over committing to a relationship, such problems are best dealt with by a psychotherapist.

By far the most common reason for retarded ejaculation is the normal aging process. As I suggested earlier, smart men view this as a positive development. The only real problems it causes are essentially side effects: a couple, especially an older one, can wear themselves out pumping away furiously to induce an orgasm, and the vagina might become irritated. Patience and a little creativity are usually enough to solve the problem. I suggest that you vary your positions and activities. Build up gradually, using less exhausting forms of stimulation, and don't hesitate to stop and rest when you need to. Also, experiment with various oils and lotions; the lubrication just might increase sensitivity enough to facilitate orgasm.

The more troubling problem, of course, is premature ejaculation—two of the most dreaded words a man can hear. They conjure up images of humiliation, failed masculinity, and frustrated women running to their vibrators. No one really knows how to define premature ejaculation. Some sex therapists define it as the inability to delay ejaculation for at least five minutes. Others take a more flexible approach, defining it as the inability to delay long enough to satisfy the woman in at least half your sexual encounters. That approach recognizes that it is normal for the time of ejaculation to vary and sometimes to fall short of the ideal.

In my opinion, it is impossible to come up with a universal definition of premature ejaculation because there is so much variation among individuals. I have met women who are perfectly satisfied with intercourse that lasts two or three minutes, while others are frustrated when their husbands can't last more than fifteen or twenty. Ultimately, it comes down to individual judgment: do you and your partner feel that you reach orgasm too quickly? If so, there are many practical steps you can take to solve the problem.

In fact, even if you *don't* have a problem, the following suggestions are worthy of your attention; they will enhance your penis power by improving your ejaculatory control, and additionally they will make your orgasms more intense.

First, let me make a few basic points. The most common

cause of premature ejaculation is quite simple: sexual inactivity. It's a matter of common sense: when the seminal vesicles are filled to capacity, it takes very little stimulation to start the ejaculation reflex; the fluid simply has to be released. This is why every man experiences quick ejaculation on occasion. It is also why it happens most often to younger men. They produce a much larger *volume* of seminal fluid, and the ejaculatory reflex is volume-related.

However, infrequent sex is not the only cause. When premature ejaculation becomes chronic it is usually because of habits rooted in early experience. For many a young man, initial sexual encounters are characterized not only by anxiety and fear, but by time pressure. He sneaks a girl into the house while his parents are out. He parks in a secluded spot where another car might show up, or even the police. He and his date duck behind a tree or into a bedroom at a party. Or he has employed the services of a prostitute who has a vested interest in the rapid turnover of clientele. Early sex can also be a solitary pursuit: teenagers who masturbate in the bathroom or under their sheets can be self-conscious to the point of paranoia; their goal is not to *delay* ejaculation, but to get it over with as quickly as possible before they're discovered.

These early experiences establish a low threshold of excitement. Most men become conditioned to ejaculate quickly. If they don't make a conscious effort to change that pattern, they can become chronic premature ejaculators. On top of that, I have often treated young men who are so humiliated by premature ejaculation that they develop a strong sense of inadequacy and shy away from sex altogether. Frequently, they compound the problem by developing erection problems as well.

Whatever the initial cause, it is important for you not to view early ejaculation as a personal failure. If it happens occasionally, it is probably due to a long lapse between orgasms. Or to nervousness; that new, passionate love affair might be so exciting that the threshold for orgasm is lowered considerably. Even if the problem is chronic, I can assure you that it is not a sign of permanent inadequacy or diminished manhood, but simply a matter of bad habits that can be changed with practice and patience.

The good news is, no matter where you start from, you can vastly increase your ejaculatory control. Using the procedures I'm about to describe, I have helped patients who reached orgasm in less than two minutes improve to where they could last more than a half hour after a few weeks or months of practice.

One point is important to make in this context: if you are in an ongoing relationship, it is important to win the support of your partner. Early ejaculation can be extremely frustrating for a woman, and if it continues for a long time it can lead to resentment. Many women have told me that they sometimes feel that their men are not even *trying* to slow down because they care only about their own needs, not the woman's. They feel used. You must convince your partner that you are sincere about improving your staying power. Tell her that you would be grateful for her patience and help. The basic goal is to delay ejaculation to a point that is most satisfying for *both* of you.

'TAIN'T EXERCISE

The following exercise, which is similar to that developed by gynecologist Arnold Kegel for female patients with urinary incontinence, will help give you greater control of your ejaculations and also increase the intensity of the orgasmic experience.

Earlier, we saw that the muscles in the perineum, the area between the scrotum and the anus, are involved in ejaculation. If you were to put your finger in that area when you ejaculate, you would feel the muscle contractions; if you placed a mirror between your legs, you would see the entire area contract like a flexing bicep. Anatomically, these muscles support the urinary sphincter, so they are the ones you contract when you are forced to hold in your urine or stop its flow. Try it the next time you urinate: when you stop the flow, the muscles you contract are the very ones we are talking about. By strengthening the perineal muscles you will pump more blood to this vital area, achieve greater ejaculatory control, and increase the intensity of your orgasms.

The basic idea is to contract and relax the muscles repeatedly, as you would in any strengthening program. You can do this either standing up or sitting down. In your mind's eye, isolate the muscle surrounding the anal sphincter. Imagine that you have inserted a rectal thermometer and are trying to pull it up into your body, right up to your Adam's apple. Don't hunch your shoulders and don't squeeze your buttocks together. The muscles involved are all internal. Squeeze them and hold that position to the count of ten. Then relax, and repeat the process several times.

As with any new exercise, the muscles will feel tired at first. Don't do it to exhaustion, but increase the number of repetitions until you can comfortably do a hundred during the course of a day. Do these exercises consistently and you will, in time, notice the benefits I described. Once you begin to notice improvement, I suggest that you continue to do the exercises to maintain the improvement and progress even further. You can do them at any time, while driving, walking, standing in line, watching TV, whatever. When done correctly, they are totally unobtrusive. If someone can see you doing them, you're doing them wrong.

A recent incident compels me to repeat one instruction. A patient to whom I taught these exercises came in a week later and said, "I've noticed an improvement, Doc, they're working great. But my asshole is sore as hell. Sticking that thermometer up there a hundred times a day is murder!" So, I repeat: *imagine* you are putting a rectal thermometer into your body.

A CHANGE OF HABIT

The key to prolonging intercourse is to become so well tuned to your own body mechanisms that you can take action to hold off ejaculation *before* it is too late. Remember, ejaculation is basically a two-step process. As arousal increases, you inevitably reach a point of no return called "ejaculatory inevitability." That's the moment when you feel that you're going to climax and there is nothing you can do about it. Physiologically speaking, you're correct: there *is* nothing you can do. Once that point is reached, the ejaculation reflex is set in motion, your perineal muscles forcefully contract, and the seminal fluid is already on its way. In seconds, the expulsion stage is triggered. To delay ejaculation you must be aware enough to do something *before* the point of inevitability sneaks up on you.

The first step is to pay close attention to physical sensations as you approach ejaculation. Just as you learned when to start braking your car as you approach a stop sign, so too you can learn to recognize when you are getting too close to the point of inevitability. That is the time to make adjustments. Some men try to distract themselves by thinking of anything besides what is going on—baseball, work, or whatever. In my experience, this is rarely effective, and even if it does slow down the process it also detracts from your full enjoyment of the moment. More effective, and far more enjoyable, is to alter the way you are thrusting at that time; changing the angle, speed, or depth of your thrusts might shift the sensations away from the head of your penis (the glans, the most sensitive part), thereby prolonging the process. Intercourse does not have to be limited to deep, rapid thrusts. You can do it slower, you can go in a circular motion, or you can enter only partway.

You can also stop thrusting entirely. Try suspending motion for a while and just lying together with your penis in her vagina. It's a great way to reduce arousal and prolong intercourse. It can also be wonderfully romantic. When you feel you can resume thrusting without ejaculating immediately, resume your motion, slowly.

Another variable is to withdraw entirely. This start-and-stop method is often used by sex therapists. When you feel yourself nearing inevitability, simply pull out and rest. If your relationship is a good one, your partner should understand the need for this and welcome the opportunity to do other erotic things. This is the time for using your hands, lips, tongue, and any other body part that gives you pleasure, while at the same time giving your penis a break from direct stimulation. When you resume intercourse, it will be that much more intense and your total time of penetration will increase. Don't be afraid of losing your erection if you stop thrusting or pull out. You *might* lose it, but so what? It will come back with the right stimulation.

SQUEEZE ME, PLEASE ME

In my experience, one of the best methods of delaying ejaculation is the "squeeze technique." When you feel close to ejaculation, withdraw. Then grip the head of your penis (the glans) at the juncture where it meets the shaft, holding your thumb on the upper surface and your first and second fingers underneath. Now squeeze forcefully. This will delay the urge to ejaculate. The amount of pressure needed varies from one man to another, but don't be afraid to squeeze hard. Your erect penis can withstand a great deal of pressure without injury. When the urge is gone, wait a moment or two before resuming intercourse. It is possible to partially lose your erection after the squeeze, but that is *usually* not a problem. If it happens, don't panic. Remain relaxed and confident, and your full erection will return shortly, especially if your penis has fresh stimulation.

The squeeze technique is time-tested. You can use it anytime you feel you are about to ejaculate. Just withdraw, squeeze, and put it back. It's what I recommend most often to my patients.

Some of my patients say they prefer to have the woman do the squeezing. I have found it more reliable for the man to do it himself, since he is more familiar with his own penis and will best know when and exactly how vigorously to squeeze. This technique is also used by my colleagues in sex therapy *without intercourse*, as a method of systematically reconditioning men with long histories of premature ejaculation. In this process, the woman stimulates the man as if masturbating him, but stops and squeezes when he signals that he is about to ejaculate. You are welcome to try this, of course, but in my experience there is nothing like on-the-job training.

THE VALSALVA MANEUVER

This technique for delaying ejaculation does not require withdrawal. The Valsalva maneuver involves holding your breath and bearing down in your abdominal area as if you were trying to eliminate stuffed bowels. You obviously squeeze your anal sphincter at the same time, of course, so you don't *actually* move your bowels. This creates a marked increase in the intra-abdominal pressure and will delay the ejaculatory mechanism. As with the squeeze technique, timing is critical. If you do it too soon it won't help; if you wait too long you might reach the point of no return and all the breath holding and squeezing in the world will be in vain. Some men continue thrusting while doing the Valsalva maneuver, while others find it more comfortable to stop for a moment until they feel they can resume without exceeding the threshold of inevitability.

If you follow the advice in this chapter you should increase your penis power batting average significantly. But please bear in mind that no matter how much you improve your self-control, there will always be moments when you ejaculate sooner than you want to. Don't get down on yourself. There is no need to feel embarrassed or ashamed. And there is no need to apologize; if you leave your partner frustrated, make up for it the next time. And when you feel yourself slip into that zone where you lose control, don't resist the inevitable; relax and enjoy it.

CLIMB TO A HIGHER ATTITUDE

Whether it is directed at your sexuality or any other aspect of your life, *self-doubt* can wilt your penis power like frost on a petal. Therefore, eliminating it should be your number one priority.

ELIMINATE NEGATIVITY AND SELF-DOUBT

A man who aspires to superpotency should not let himself succumb to negativity in any form. Of course you're not perfect. Of course you make mistakes. Of course you have weak spots and insecurities. We all do. I am not advocating denial. But a superpotent man faces his imperfections with honesty and humor, and never lets anything obscure his basic, unconditional acceptance of himself.

If you see the proverbial glass as half full rather than half empty, your penis will *behave* like it's full. But if you succumb to cynicism, negativity, and despair, you will become an empty shell and so will your penis. Every situation, sexual or otherwise, can be seen in a multitude of ways. It's up to you to interpret reality in a way that reinforces your self-esteem.

Act like a winner in life and you will be a winner in bed. Face the world with courage and your penis will be courageous as well. Go through life with a smile on your face and your penis will smile too. Extract every drop of pleasure that life offers you and your penis will make you doubly happy.

It might take time and effort to cultivate the positive attitudes necessary for superpotency. Old habits are hard to break, and negative thinking *is* a habit. Your mind might be accustomed to focusing on the bad because it is afraid of letting its guard down. Some of us learned early on that if we expect too much we end up disappointed or ambushed by fate. We learned to look for the negative as a kind of self-defense. Too often I have seen negativity become a self-fulfilling prophecy. The trick is to see reality for what it is, but focus on your own positive traits and have confidence in your ability to make the most out of any situation. I guarantee that if you do this your penis power will flourish.

DON'T VIEW SEX AS PERFORMANCE

As I've pointed out repeatedly, anxiety over performance is a sure bet to produce penis weakness. If you stop thinking about sex as something you perform, as if it were a stage production or an athletic event, you won't have that performance anxiety. If you find yourself thinking about how you are going to do when you are in bed, you are on the wrong track. Alter the image immediately. Visualize yourself simply enjoying each and every moment of the anticipated sexual encounter. Go into it expecting nothing from yourself other than to experience pleasure and give pleasure to your partner. Don't sweat whether you're doing okay or how you compare to other men. Remove all such comparisons and all standards of performance from your mind. Take it as it comes.

The outcome does not matter. What matters is your capacity to relax and enjoy the moment. Your attitude toward your penis should be the same as what it would be toward a child who was playing a soccer game or taking an exam: "I don't care if you win or lose. All that matters is that you give it your best shot."

And never let yourself be intimidated by a sexual partner. If she is too demanding, if her expectations are unrealistic, if she compares you to other men, the problem is *hers*, not yours. Never let such an attitude inhibit you or make you fret over your performance. Yes, you have a responsibility to do your best to satisfy your partner, but all you can do is exactly that: give it your best effort. If you've done that, you have nothing to feel guilty or ashamed of; such emotions don't belong in the life of a superpotent man.

MAKE FRIENDS WITH YOUR PENIS

At least as much as any other part of your body, your penis is out there representing you, reflecting what you think of yourself and the world. Love your penis. Respect it, treat it well, take pride in it. Above all, have faith in it. Your penis is your friend; treat it accordingly.

I don't care how big or small it is, what it looks like, or how it's performed for you in the past. If your penis has let you down at any point and you have come to mistrust it, forgive it, forget it, and move on. Take responsibility for previous failures; don't attribute them to your penis. It is only an emissary, following orders from your brain. Don't kill the messenger. Your penis will behave the way you want it to if you treat it well and let it know you believe in it.

I can't emphasize this enough. Nothing will invigorate you more than an enthusiastic attitude toward your penis. If doubts about it pop into your mind, challenge them. Redirect your thoughts. Tell yourself, "My penis has my utmost confidence and support. It is my friend. It will serve me faithfully."

Spend some time alone with your penis. I don't necessarily mean to masturbate, I mean take a good look at it in the mirror and see it for the beautiful, whimsical organ it is. It's a court jester and a sage rolled into one. It wants only to bring you happiness. Touch it, massage it with lotion, sprinkle it with fragrance. There is no reason men should be ashamed of doing such things. We treat our faces and the rest of our bodies with special care, so why not our genitals? Doing this will help fortify the bond between your brain and your penis. Treat your penis with respect and it will serve you with dignity.

A FINAL WORD TO WOMEN

That last sentence can be paraphrased for women: treat his penis with respect and it will serve you with dignity. This chapter has been directed to men, but I sincerely hope that women will study it carefully and use the information to help their partners become superpotent. As I stated earlier, women who know how to attend to their men's penises have better relationships and better sex. I firmly believe that if you take some of the time you spend trying to look attractive to men and use it to directly satisfy their penis needs, you will attain far greater fulfillment.

Knowing how easily such statements can be misconstrued, and how sensitive matters between the sexes are these days, I must emphasize: being a penis-oriented woman does not make you less than an equal to the men in your life. Taking the trouble to understand what makes your man tick and learning to satisfy his needs does not make you in any way subservient. It simply means holding up your end of the bargain so that *your* needs are satisfied in return. By taking the initiative, you can establish a precedent that your man can be expected to follow, quid pro quo.

More than twenty years of clinical experience have convinced me of this: an intelligent woman knows that one of the best ways to a man's heart and soul is through his penis.

A FINAL WORD TO MEN

Penis power is not about size, and it's not about blood vessels and nerves. Rather, it's about heightened self-awareness. It's about an enlightened attitude that is enthusiastic, conciliatory, and understandingly assertive. It is about admiring and respecting a body part that is never out of style and can never be overused or worn out. It is about letting your penis read your mind, and allowing your mind's voice to cry out, "My penis is *great,* and if it's great, *I'm* great!"

Penis power is a priceless luxury that is readily available to every man, to be shared by every woman throughout a lifetime of intimacy and compassion. Penis power is not about domination; it's about communication and sensitivity between lovers. It is about sharing the mystique of man's most enigmatic body part with an understanding, enthusiastic partner. Penis power is about generosity and sharing—not out of a need to achieve saintliness but for enlightened self-interest. The more you give, the more you get back.

Penis power is about reducing anxiety and enhancing the quality of your life in every respect. It is about maintaining good health, exercise, diet, and attitude. It is about appreciating the penis you have, instead of having a penis you don't appreciate. It is realizing that your penis is God's gift, but that penis power is your own personal achievement—to be shared wisely with your mate, so that together you can soar to new heights of pleasure, richness, and intimacy.

As a penis doctor, I recommend that you stay as young as your penis. Develop your penis communication skills. Do not lose faith in the perfectability of the human penis. Love as well as you can, because to love well is to live well. Share the pleasures of your penis as honestly and openly as you can and you and your partner will be better off for it. Life is about more than eating and drinking, getting and spending. It's about cultivating a healthy body and a healthy mind. And that is the essence of superpotency.

I truly believe that a wise man would rather be a pauper and use his penis like a king, than be a king who is incapable of exercising and sharing his God-given right to penis power.

INDEX